WORKING
SCARED

August, 1993

To Jon & family —

  It has been my pleasure
knowing and working with you
over the years. I wish you the
best of everything —

       Ken

Kenneth N. Wexley
Stanley B. Silverman

WORKING SCARED

ACHIEVING
SUCCESS
IN TRYING TIMES

Jossey-Bass Publishers · San Francisco

Substantial discounts on bulk quantities of Jossey-Bass books are available to corporations, professional associations, and other organizations. For details and discount information, contact the special sales department at Jossey-Bass Inc., Publishers. (415) 433-1740; Fax (415) 433-0499.

For sales outside the United States, contact Maxwell Macmillan International Publishing Group, 866 Third Avenue, New York, New York 10022.

Manufactured in the United States of America

The paper used in this book is acid-free and meets the State of California requirements for recycled paper (50 percent recycled waste, including 10 percent postconsumer waste), which are the strictest guidelines for recycled paper currently in use in the United States.

10% POST CONSUMER WASTE

The ink in this book is either soy- or vegetable-based and during the printing process emits fewer than half the volatile organic compounds (VOCs) emitted by petroleum-based ink.

Library of Congress Cataloging-in-Publication Data

Wexley, Kenneth N., date.
    Working scared : achieving success in trying times / Kenneth N. Wexley, Stanley B. Silverman. — 1st ed.
        p.   cm. — (The Jossey-Bass management series)
    Includes bibliographical references and index.
    ISBN 1-55542-512-7 (alk. paper)
    1. Success in business—United States.   2. Career development—United States.   I. Silverman, Stanley B., date.   II. Title.
III. Series.
HF5386.W456   1993
650.1—dc20   92-39967
                                                                                    CIP

FIRST EDITION
HB Printing   10 9 8 7 6 5 4 3 2 1   *Code 9321*

THE JOSSEY-BASS
MANAGEMENT SERIES

Contents

Preface   xi

The Authors   xv

Prologue: Uncovering Your Concerns, Anxieties,
and Fears   1

1. Thriving with Less Supervision   7

2. Collaborating in a Team Culture   22

3. Succeeding in a Quality-Focused Organization   45

4. Surviving During a Downsizing   73

5. Staying Flexible During Mergers and Acquisitions   89

6. Working with Diverse Co-Workers   109

7. Making the Most of an Overseas Assignment   131

8. Sharing the Gains of the New Pay Strategies   161

Summary: The Six Keys for Success in Trying Times   175

Notes   177

Index   185

For
Ruthie, David, Matthew, Sheri, and Mom
Zippy, Lindsay, Ryan, Sam, Anne, Laura, and Dad

Preface

We have been working as human resource consultants to large and small organizations for almost twenty-five years. During this time, we've had the pleasure of collaborating with managers and employees at all levels, from the executive boardroom to the factory floor. We've provided our clients with services in the areas of management development, performance management and appraisal, organization development, employee training, and personnel selection.

Lately, we've begun to notice a great unrest among employees in many American organizations. At first, we thought that the unhappiness we were seeing was restricted to a few unique companies. However, over time, we've come to realize that these feelings of uneasiness, fear, uncertainty, and worry are quite pervasive. About three years ago, we began to refer to these feelings in the workplace as "working scared." We also noted that once employees begin working scared, they function less effectively in their jobs. We don't know exactly how many Americans are, in fact, working scared, but we do know that, with all the turbulent changes in our society, they are a large percentage of the American work force.

Using This Book

We've written this book to try to help those American employees and managers who are now working scared, or are fearful that they will be soon. It makes no difference who you are or what your position is within your company. The only thing that matters is that you are experiencing discomfort right now or are worried that you will in the near future. We decided that this syndrome is eating away at the core feelings and values of American employees, and that something had to be done.

For the past two years, we've interviewed large numbers of people who know this feeling, from either their own experience or observing others who are working scared. Based on everything we learned from them, plus our own consulting experiences, we concluded that there are things that employees and their managers can do to cope with fear and achieve greater success. We've taken all these strategies and put them into *Working Scared*.

Success in Eight Dimensions

Based on our interviews, we've determined that there are eight main reasons why American employees are working scared, eight trends in business that create fear in people. Not that these are the only reasons for feelings of fear and uneasiness; we're certain that you will be able to think of others. Nevertheless, we've chosen what we believe are the most critical areas that you will need to be concerned about now and in the years ahead. They are:

- Reduced supervision
- Team culture
- Quality focus
- Downsizing
- Mergers and acquisitions
- Increasing diversity
- Overseas assignment
- Innovative pay strategies

In the chapters ahead you're going to get a greater understanding of each of these eight areas. You're also going to be provided practical solutions that you can use immediately on your job. With them, you won't have to continue working

scared; you'll be able to achieve success in spite of today's trying times.

A Real-World Perspective

Every incident described in this book is a real-world experience
that we have personally observed or been told about. Nothing
has been fabricated. In each chapter, we start off by giving you
the facts about the issue so that you can get a feel for the importance of the topic. Next, we present a story — a *real* story.
The only things we've changed are the names of the actual organizations and the individuals involved. Finally, we'll present
solutions that we have seen implemented successfully. The solutions are divided into two groups: those that are directed toward
employees, those that are more appropriate for managers. Of
course there is much overlap.

Each chapter also presents success pointers — practical tips
that you can apply immediately: tips to help employees cope
with their own situations, and tips that managers can use to
help people become more successful.

Regardless of whether you're a manager or an employee,
we highly recommend that you read both perspectives. Why?
As a manager, don't forget that you are also an employee. And,
as an employee, it pays for you to be knowledgeable about the
kinds of things your manager can do for you. In fact, some of
the strategies that we suggest are things that you might pass
along to your manager.

The strategies we suggest are not the only possible ones,
but simply those we consider the best. We also realize that certain strategies can help in many different situations. Rather than
being redundant, we decided to place each in the one chapter
where we felt it had the greatest benefit.

Acknowledgments

We'd like to begin by thanking all those people who told us,
"Please don't mention my name or the name of my company."
You know who you are, and we'll always be grateful to you for

the time you gave us and the discomfort you endured in relaying your painful experiences.

We also owe a great deal of thanks to the following people: Mark Bobes, Goodyear Tire and Rubber; Dallas Burdick, Lansing Board of Water and Light; Howard Campbell, Sparrow Hospital; Georgia Chao, Michigan State University; Phillip DeVries; Colleen Frayne, University of Western Ontario; Stanley Glauberman, Malco Products Inc.; Kenneth Glickman, Right Associates; Suzanne Hendler; Cathy Higgs, Allstate Insurance Company; Nick Horney, Stouffer Hotels and Resorts; Dave Houghton, Industrial Metal Products, Inc.; Alison Howie-Day, Lansing Board of Water and Light; Sherry Hoy, Chase Manhattan Bank; Robert Juran; Carrie Knapp, Wells Fargo Bank; Arno Kolz; Mike Lovett, Piedmont Associated Industries; Richard Manwaring, General Motors; Chris Marlin, Tenneco Automotive; Carol Moore; Mark Newton, Chrysler Corporation; Susan Palmer, Wells Fargo Bank; James Rucker, General Motors; Joan Rucker; Brenda Somers; Steven Somers, General Motors; Scott Spera, AT&T; Rick Steinberg, Computer Task Group; Eric Stevens; Jim Switzer, University of Akron; and Deborah Winters.

Last, but never least, we'd like to say thanks to our families. They had to tolerate our feelings of "writing scared" as we struggled to meet our editors', Bill Hicks's and Frank Welsch's, schedule. They also read our chapters and made valuable contributions to the final version. Thanks to Bill, Frank, and the entire Jossey-Bass team for being so professional.

With love and thanks,

January 1993   Kenneth N. Wexley
                                                     Okemos, Michigan

                                                     Stanley B. Silverman
                                                     Akron, Ohio

The Authors

Kenneth N. Wexley is currently a managing partner with Human Resource Decisions, Inc. He earned his B.A. degree (1965) from the State University of New York, Buffalo, in psychology, his M.A. degree (1966) from Temple University in psychology, and his Ph.D. degree (1969) from the University of Tennessee in industrial and organizational psychology.

Wexley has done extensive consulting and research work in the field of human resource management with particular emphasis on performance appraisal, management and supervisory development, and personnel selection. For over twenty years, he has been a consultant to many organizations, such as AT&T, Bridgestone U.S.A., General Motors, Goodyear Tire & Rubber, Knight-Ridder Newspapers, the Lansing Board of Water and Light, Michigan Bell, Shell Chemical, and Sparrow Hospital.

He is the author of more than fifty professional articles on human resource management practices. He has written numerous books including *Developing Human Resources* (1991), *Developing and Training Human Resources in Organizations* (1991), *Increasing Productivity Through Performance Appraisal,* (1981), and *Organizational Behavior and Industrial Psychology* (1975). He has been, through his long career, a professor at the University of Akron, Michigan State University, and the University of California, Berkeley. He has also been a guest lecturer at the University of Sheffield in England.

Wexley has been named a fellow of the American Psychological Association for his outstanding research contributions. He has also been awarded diplomate status by the American

Board of Professional Psychology. In addition, he has recently
served as chair of the personnel and human resource division
of the Academy of Management.

Stanley B. Silverman is currently a full professor at the University of Akron and a managing partner with Human Resource
Decisions, Inc. He received his B.S. degree (1970) from Ohio
State University in psychology and his M.A. degree (1973) from
Middle Tennessee State University in industrial and organizational psychology. For over fifteen years he has been actively
involved in human resource consulting and personnel research
with a wide variety of organizations. He has extensive experience in the field of human resource management, with particular emphasis in training and management development, test vali-
dation and personnel selection, performance appraisal, attitude
surveys, employment interviewing, and assessment centers.

He has most recently been involved in the design and development of performance management and appraisal systems
and corresponding training programs for many organizations.
He has published articles on performance appraisal, personnel
selection, and job analysis in *The Journal of Applied Psychology,
Personnel Psychology, Public Personnel Management,* and *Personnel Assessment Monographs.* He recently completed a book chapter on
individual development and performance management and appraisal for a handbook series published by SHRM/BNA Books.
Silverman has been working with many small and medium-sized
companies as well as with some of the largest corporations in
the world. His many clients have included: Allstate, American
Can Company, AT&T, B. F. Goodrich, Babcock & Wilcox,
Coca-Cola USA, General Motors, Goodyear Tire and Rubber,
Knight-Ridder Newspapers, and Ohio Edison.

Silverman has been very active nationally in division 14
(Society for Industrial and Organizational Psychology, Inc.) of
the American Psychological Association, where he has chaired
national conventions and various committees. He recently returned from Kyoto, Japan, where he presented his work on performance management and appraisal at the 22nd International
Congress of Applied Psychology.

WORKING
SCARED

Prologue

Uncovering Your
Concerns, Anxieties, and Fears

"Working scared" has become an all too familiar feeling among American employees. As the world economic situation changes, and companies change to keep up and remain competitive, a climate of fear often takes over. In all kinds of organizations, people at all levels are feeling nervous and uneasy about their jobs—they are working scared.

What is happening to American jobs? The turbulent times we live in have created eight major areas of change in our organizations, each with its own challenges.

• *Less supervision.* As organizations cut back on the number of managers and supervisors, the remaining managers have more employees reporting to them and aren't able to give them as much time. Although there are some who enjoy less supervision, a great many employees feel uncomfortable with this situation; they're not sure whether they're accomplishing what their managers expect of them and don't receive the guidance they would like.

• *Team culture.* There was a time when American employees worked pretty much on their own. Sure, they were expected to help out co-workers occasionally, but by and large they functioned as individual contributors. Nowadays, employees of all kinds—factory workers, service people, technical staffers, supervisors, and managers—are expected to work in a team environment. Although they may have participated in various types

1

of teams in their personal lives (such as sports and volunteer groups), many find it difficult to function as an effective team player at work.

- *Focus on quality.* A great many American organizations are realizing that in order to survive, they have to become more quality-focused. This is having a major impact on the jobs of many American workers, who are forced to learn new concepts and tools to increase the quality of their work.

- *Downsizing.* Layoffs, cutbacks, retrenchment, reduction in force—whatever we call it, downsizing is an issue that won't go away. The prevalence of cutbacks and retrenchments in many industries has increased in recent years. Our economy has caused many organizations to conclude that they must get "lean and mean" if they are to survive. So large numbers of American workers are working scared, fearing that they might be the next to go.

- *Mergers and acquisitions.* Pick up any magazine or newspaper today and you're bound to read about two companies that are combining (merger) or one company that is "gobbling up" another (acquisition). The new company that results after a merger or an acquisition differs greatly, in many ways, from the old ones, and every single person within the organization is affected.

- *Increasingly diverse work force.* The American work force is steadily becoming more and more diverse in nature. We can no longer assume that our co-workers will have backgrounds similar to ours. For many American employees, working collaboratively with others who are culturally different can be scary.

- *International environment.* There's a fair chance that you may be offered the opportunity to work for your organization in another country for a while. Some consider an international assignment exciting; many see it as scary, especially if it means uprooting their family for several years. Coping in a foreign country is stressful; returning home is not always an easy adjustment.

• *Innovative pay strategies.* We will also experience, in the years ahead, changes in the way we are remunerated. Regular paychecks based on straight salaries or number of hours worked or number of units produced are becoming a thing of the past.

All these changes create a sense of fear, of helplessness. Being scared isn't pleasant. Working scared interferes with your ability to be successful at your job. But there are ways to cope, and that's what this book is all about. You will learn specific things you can do in each of the eight problem areas. First, though, let's find out what's happening in your particular job. Take a few minutes to complete the Working Scared Survey.

Working Scared Survey

		Yes	No
1.	Are you clear on your major responsibilities and which ones are most important?	☐	☐
2.	Do you know what it takes to be a successful team player?	☐	☐
3.	Do you know how to enhance quality on your job?	☐	☐
4.	Have you been able to let rumors about downsizing not bother you?	☐	☐
5.	Do you know how to reduce your stress or uncertainty in the event of a merger or acquisition?	☐	☐
6.	Do you understand your own values and prejudices toward people who are different from you?	☐	☐
7.	Do you know what to do when your pay is tied to the financial fortunes of your organization?	☐	☐
8.	Do you know how pay strategies will change in the future?	☐	☐
9.	Are you clear on your manager's performance expectations of you?	☐	☐
10.	Do you have an understanding of how teams develop and change over time?	☐	☐
11.	Do you know what total quality management (TQM) is?	☐	☐
12.	Do you know how to remain positive in the face of company downsizing?	☐	☐
13.	Do you know how your job might change if your organization merged or was acquired?	☐	☐

		Yes	No
14.	Do you know how to work effectively with people who are culturally different from you?	☐	☐
15.	Are you aware of the difference between American cultural values and those of other countries?	☐	☐
16.	Do you have a clear idea of how you can improve your job performance?	☐	☐
17.	Are you aware of the responsibilities of self-managed work team members?	☐	☐
18.	Do you know who your customers are?	☐	☐
19.	Would you be able to set effective goals to remain productive during a merger or acquisition?	☐	☐
20.	Are you aware of what you need to do once you arrive in the new country to make your international assignment successful?	☐	☐
21.	Do you know why your pay may be more variable or uneven in the future?	☐	☐
22.	Do you receive enough feedback about your job performance?	☐	☐
23.	Do you know how to maintain open communications to ensure a high-performing work team?	☐	☐
24.	Do you know how to foster teamwork?	☐	☐
25.	Do you know what customers expect of you?	☐	☐
26.	Do you know when to stay and when to leave, if a merger or acquisition occurred in your organization?	☐	☐
27.	Do you know what personal attributes you need to be successful in an international assignment?	☐	☐
28.	Do you have a clear idea of how your work performance will affect your pay in the future?	☐	☐
29.	Are you aware of the critical issues that you will face when you return home from an international assignment?	☐	☐
30.	Does the management in your organization support the value of cultural diversity?	☐	☐
31.	Do you know how to guard against becoming a victim of company downsizing?	☐	☐
32.	Do you know how to use various tools for improving quality?	☐	☐
33.	Do you know how to handle counterproductive members of your work team?	☐	☐

	Yes	No
34. Do you know what things you should consider before accepting an international assignment?	□	□
35. Do you know how to make yourself more valuable to your organization in the midst of downsizing?	□	□

Now let's interpret your answers in light of the eight performance areas. Look back at the survey and transfer your answers here.

Less Supervision

Question 1: _____
Question 9: _____
Question 16: _____
Question 22: _____

Team Culture

Question 2: _____
Question 10: _____
Question 17: _____
Question 23: _____
Question 24: _____
Question 33: _____

Focus on Quality

Question 3: _____
Question 11: _____
Question 18: _____
Question 25: _____
Question 32: _____

Downsizing

Question 4: _____
Question 12: _____
Question 31: _____
Question 35: _____

Mergers and Acquisitions

Question 5: _____
Question 13: _____
Question 19: _____
Question 26: _____

Increasingly Diverse Work Force

Question 6: _____
Question 14: _____
Question 30: _____

International Environment

Question 15: _____
Question 20: _____
Question 27: _____
Question 29: _____
Question 34: _____

Innovative Pay Strategies

Question 7: _____
Question 8: _____
Question 21: _____
Question 28: _____

Now look at your answers. A "no" signals that you are feeling ill at ease about your work situation in that area. You may have "no's" in more than one area — like millions of others in the American work force.

This book will help you reduce the uncomfortable feeling of working scared. In the chapters that follow, you will learn more about these eight important areas, and how to be successful in spite of them. Each chapter presents:

- The facts about the issue.
- The story of one or more employees who face the situation (the names have been changed, of course).
- Solutions from the viewpoint of employees and managers — what employees can do to improve their current situation, and what managers can do to help people work more effectively.

ONE

Thriving with
Less Supervision

Working scared has become a way of life for many people because they are getting less direction from their managers than they did just a few years ago. They're not sure whether they're accomplishing what their managers expect of them. They feel that they're out there all alone. What's more, many experts agree that this trend of receiving less supervision will continue.

What's happening? The number of managers is shrinking. A few years ago, an individual might have shared a manager with four or five other employees; today that person has to share that same manager with thirty people. Within the last decade, the average number of employees reporting to a manager at Xerox Corporation and at General Electric has doubled.[1] The reason for this trend is that many organizations are stripping away layers of middle-level management. A decade ago at General Electric there were ten management layers between the CEO and the folks on the plant floor, whereas today there are only five.[2] Several years ago, at Eastman Kodak, thirteen levels of management separated the senior vice president of manufacturing from the factory floor; now that vice president is just four levels from production.[3] These companies are not alone. Ford, 3M, Westinghouse Electric, Hewlett-Packard, Apple Computer, Goodyear Tire & Rubber, Dana Corporation, Federal Express, Motorola, and many more are doing the same.

What do these organizations hope to get out of this? For one thing, they expect to cut costs by operating with fewer managers and giving those who remain greater responsibility. They believe that many managers are underused and that each manager could easily handle more employees. Second, they also expect to boost efficiency by having faster and more accurate communications. Finally, they hope to create an atmosphere with less psychological distance between workers and executives.

Pat's Story

Summit Corporation is a large manufacturer of hand-held computers. These computers are sold to two main types of customers: restaurant chains, where they are used by waiters and waitresses when taking food and beverage orders, and retail establishments, such as department and clothing stores, for inventory control. Last year, Summit's sales and customer service division was reorganized and one management layer was eliminated.

A year ago, there were three levels of management separating the vice president of sales and customer service from the customer service representatives: the director of customer service at the top, then the regional customer service managers, and then the customer service supervisors. Then Summit eliminated the middle layer. Before the reorganization, five supervisors reported to each regional manager; today all twenty of these supervisors report directly to the company's director of customer service.

Soon after Clark Johnson, the vice president of sales and customer service, made the decision to streamline the organization, he said, "I believe that this streamlining of our sales and customer service organization will bring about tremendous cost savings and result in a leaner, more efficient operation. As you know, I'm a strong believer that layer reduction will not work in all organizations. Nevertheless, after reviewing the final report written by an outside management consulting firm, I am convinced that we can remove the regional customer service manager level without any detrimental effects on our organization."

Pat Williams is one of the twenty supervisors who now report directly to Terry Grant, the director of customer service. Up until last year, Pat met every week with the regional manager she reported to; these weekly meetings gave Pat direction, feedback, and a feeling of security. She doesn't have the same close working relationship with her new manager.

Pat Williams is working scared. Yesterday, she had her yearly performance review with Terry Grant. She left the session feeling anxious about her future at Summit Corporation. For one thing, Pat found that she and Terry had very different ideas about what she is expected to accomplish. Up to now she has been spending the least amount of her time providing direction and support to the customer service representatives she supervises. Yesterday, Terry made it very clear for the first time that he believes this is one of Pat's major responsibilities and that she has not been giving it enough attention. Pat was also upset when Terry informed her that she needs to keep him more fully informed of customer complaints. This was particularly distressing because Pat feels she has been doing a good job of keeping Terry informed.

Pat left the performance review session feeling that she is in a no-win situation. She realizes that Terry is busy, but, at the same time, she believes that it's unfair to not hear about his expectations until her performance review. She wants to do a better job of keeping Terry informed about customer complaints, but doesn't understand what Terry wants her to do differently. In short, Pat feels that she needs Terry's help but realizes that he doesn't have time to spend with her.

Strategies for Employees

Pat and Terry have different ideas about what Pat is supposed to be doing. This is not surprising. Quite often, when organizations are delayered, communications between employees and their managers tend to break down and confusion results. If you found yourself in Pat's situation, what could you do to eliminate your anxiety and achieve success? The answer lies in these three success strategies:

1.   Clarify major job responsibilities.
2.   Clarify performance expectations.
3.   Seek feedback.

Clarify Major Job Responsibilities

Get a snapshot. The first thing to do is to get a "snapshot" of what your job consists of now. Most jobs can be broken down into about five to ten major responsibilities, each including a cluster of job duties that you accomplish on a regular basis.

For example, let's consider Pat's job. A customer service supervisor has six major responsibilities:

1. Maintain customer relations
2. Maintain employee relations
3. Cooperate with other departments
4. Monitor computerized billing and credit system
5. Recruit and select customer service representatives
6. Administer company policies and procedures

Ask what's most important. Once the snapshot is taken, it's critical to think about the relative importance of the major responsibilities. After all, the importance of each responsibility should influence the amount of effort that you expend on it.

A simple way to prioritize major responsibilities is to take 100 points and distribute them across the responsibilities. For instance, Pat's list might look like this:

1. Maintain customer relations (30 points)
2. Maintain employee relations (20 points)
3. Cooperate with other departments (10 points)
4. Monitor computerized billing and credit system (20 points)
5. Recruit and select customer service representatives (10 points)
6. Administer company policies and procedures (10 points)

This weighting clarifies the fact that maintaining good customer relations is the most important aspect of Pat's job, closely followed by maintaining employee relations and monitoring the computerized billing and credit system. It is clear that the remaining three responsibilities are not as important to job success.

Involve your manager. It is vital that you and your manager agree on the major responsibilities of your job and also on their relative importance. A very good approach is for you to work on determining your responsibilities and their weightings on your own, and then show them to your manager. This creates a good forum for discussion and leads to reconciling any differences and clarifying your job. If Pat and Terry had done this, Pat's frustrations would never have occurred.

Clarify Performance Expectations

Getting agreement on what makes for success. Agreeing with your manager as to your major responsibilities is only the initial step. You also need to agree on what constitutes success in those areas. To do this, you and your manager must agree on a minimum of five performance expectations for each major responsibility.

Performance expectations describe good, effective levels of performance for a given major responsibility. The expectations specify how your work is to be done and what you are to accomplish. They define the methods, behaviors, or actions you need to use in performing a particular major responsibility, and the outcomes that you are expected to achieve. Outcomes should be results that can actually be measured, in quantity, quality, or timeliness.

Let's use Pat's job as an example. One of her major responsibilities—maintain employee relations—might include these four performance expectations:

1. Spend at least four hours per week working directly with the customer service representatives.
2. Invite customer service representatives' input before deciding on issues that will directly affect them.
3. Provide customer service representatives with new product information within two days of receiving it.
4. Clarify with each employee what is expected with regard to major responsibilities and performance expectations.

Make sure your expectations are well conceived. Good performance expectations have several characteristics: they are under the employee's control, important to job success, challenging but not impossible, and measurable or observable. In addition, they should not be phrased in terms of personality traits because those are much too vague. For instance, suppose initiative is important to success on your job. The appropriate performance expectation is not the trait itself, but rather what you should do to show initiative; for example, "work overtime without being asked when a deadline approaches."

Involve your manager again. Just as you developed your major responsibilities by yourself and then discussed them with your manager, follow the same process with your performance expectations. Too often employees bemoan the fact that they do not have a clear idea what their managers expect of them. On several occasions, Pat has vented her frustration to other supervisors by saying, "I have no idea what Terry expects of me. I can only hope that we're on the same wavelength." If they had done these two steps, Pat wouldn't have to hope—she would know.

Unless these first two strategies are carefully undertaken, achieving success is like groping in the dark. How can we ever expect to eliminate anxiety and achieve success when the path to success is never really paved?

Seek Feedback

People who are working scared because of so little supervision need to actively seek out feedback from others, such as managers, co-workers, subordinates, and customers. That feedback will allow you to make continual improvements in your own performance. It also helps you sustain high levels of job motivation and satisfaction. When you work with other people, you cannot ignore how they see your job performance. Any differences between your opinion and theirs should be discussed and resolved.

To use feedback to your maximum advantage, you need to ensure that this feedback is of the highest quality. Here are some key pointers.

Keep the focus on major responsibilities and performance expecta-

tions. Often, when your manager or a co-worker is dissatisfied with how you are performing, you will be compared unfavorably with other employees. It's not only disturbing, it's also not very informative—it tells you nothing about how you can improve your performance.

To get quality feedback in this situation, you need to steer the conversation away from comparisons with others and toward your own major responsibilities and performance expectations.

Seek out feedback on a continual basis. Don't wait until your end-of-the-year performance review to find out how you are doing. You certainly don't want feedback saved up and dumped on you all at one time. Instead, take it upon yourself to meet periodically with your manager to discuss how you are doing on each of your major responsibilities. You will recall from our story that Pat heard things at the end of the year that she had never heard before. This situation would never have occurred if Pat had sought regular feedback from Terry and others.

Besides your manager, anyone inside or outside your organization who is in a position to observe your performance on one or more of your major responsibilities can supply you with meaningful feedback. This could include people from other departments that you work with regularly, co-workers, or even customers.

Seek feedback in terms of behaviors or results. Don't settle for feedback that characterizes your job performance in terms of personal traits such as:

"You're too aggressive."
"You need to be more of a self-starter."
"You are not a good enough team player."

Comments like these are usually not personal attacks, but merely the person's lack of skill at describing the situation. Try to turn these comments into opportunities for improvement. Ask the individual, "What have you seen me doing or not doing that makes you say that I am too aggressive?" By asking this question, you encourage the person to be more specific and to discuss the behaviors or results that you are not accomplishing.

If you are serious about seeking quality feedback, you will get both positives and negatives. We all like hearing positive feedback about ourselves, and there is nothing wrong with seeking out positive feedback. But the truth is that gathering developmental feedback through the three pointers just discussed is what will really help you achieve greater success.

EMPLOYEE SUCCESS POINTERS
Achieving Success with Less Supervision

➤ Think through your job and come up with five to ten major responsibilities.

➤ Decide which responsibilities are the most critical to your job success.

➤ Define effective performance for each major responsibility through performance expectations.

➤ Make certain that your performance expectations include effective results and behaviors.

➤ Meet with your manager to reach consensus on your major responsibilities and performance expectations.

➤ Each month, compare your current level of performance with your performance expectations.

➤ Seek high-quality feedback on a continual basis from others such as managers, co-workers, your employees, and customers.

➤ Don't limit yourself to only positive feedback but, more important, seek out developmental feedback.

Strategies for Managers

We know that managers in today's flatter organizations are extremely busy. You, as a manager, may have a span of control that is much larger than it was previously. There are solutions. Some can make your job easier right away; others may seem like more work initially but they will make your job easier in the long run.

Delegate More

Because you are probably extremely busy, you must start thinking about those aspects of your job that can be delegated to others. One way of doing this is to follow this three-step process:

Step 1: Write down your own major responsibilities and begin thinking about the various duties associated with them.

Step 2: Indicate with an *A, B,* or *C* how critical it is that a particular major responsibility remain under your control.

        A = Is a critical component of my job and must remain that way.

        B = Is important to my job as a manager, but aspects of it could be delegated to my staff.

        C = Is a major responsibility that could be delegated entirely to others.

Step 3: Analyze the *B* and *C* responsibilities and delegate them to the appropriate people. Ask yourself:

    1. Who has the interest in this responsibility?
    2. Who has the time to do it?
    3. Who has the skills and abilities to do it?

Support the Three Success Strategies

Review the three success strategies for employees described in the previous section: clarify major responsibilities, clarify performance expectations, and seek feedback. To help your employees accomplish these strategies, and therefore make yourself more successful as a manager in the long run, you must support the process and participate in it. Meet with your employees to define and agree upon the relative importance of their various responsibilities and to clarify what you expect of them. You must also be willing to meet with your employees on a regular basis to give them the amount of feedback they need to remain motivated.

But what happens when employees are not meeting their agreed-upon expectations? It is your job to step in and become a coach.

Coach and Develop Employees

Even though you may be extremely busy, it is important that you have a systematic process in place that allows you to coach and develop your employees when they are having performance problems. The four-phase coaching and development cycle, illustrated in Figure 1.1, is one recommended process.

Figure 1.1. Four-Phase Coaching and Development Cycle.

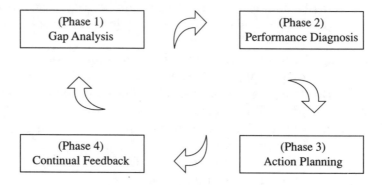

Source: *Appraising and Developing Employee Performance Training (ADEPT)* (Akron, OH: Human Resource Decisions, Inc., 1988). Reprinted with permission.

Phase 1: Conduct Gap Analysis. Once major job responsibilities and performance expectations are set, you are able to compare an employee's expectations against current performance. Gap analysis is the strategy for making this comparison.

When an employee is having a problem accomplishing a critical aspect of the job, gap analysis can help pinpoint the problem. Review the performance expectations within the major responsibility where there are problems, and then compare them with the current level of performance. Your objective is to identify any gaps that might exist. Only when you have carefully identified these gaps can you hope to improve your employee's current level of performance.

Let's go back to Pat's position as a customer service supervisor. The major responsibility is maintaining employee relations, and one performance expectation for that area is "spend at least four hours per week working directly with the customer service representatives." Terry, her manager, did a gap analysis.

Expected Performance –	*Current Performance* =	*Gap*
Spend at least four hours per week working with customer service reps	Averages 1 hour per week working with customer service reps	3 hours

Once Terry identifies a gap between current and expected performance, he needs to meet with Pat, explain the fact that the gap exists, and work with her to determine the cause — phase two.

Phase 2: Conduct Performance Diagnosis. Causes of performance blocks can be found in four possible areas:

1. Factors outside the organization
2. Factors inside the organization
3. The manager
4. The employee

Outside factors are those things that occur outside the job and the company but nevertheless can affect job performance: local economic conditions, governmental regulations, supply shortages, defective raw materials, and new competition, for example. You might not be able to do much about some of these outside factors, but it certainly helps to understand them.

Events that occur inside your organization, not related to you or your employee, can also affect job performance. Examples include such things as organizational changes, physical working conditions, company policies and procedures, and poor communications.

You, the manager, may also be a major factor in influencing your employee's job performance. You might not provide adequate training, give enough positive feedback, make it clear enough what is expected of them, or share important organizational goals with your employees.

Finally, the employee himself or herself is also a critical influence on performance. Performance problems can be caused by:

- Can't do's
- Won't do's
- Don't know what to do's

The "can't do's" represent a performance problem caused by a lack of job knowledge, poor interpersonal skills, or weak technical abilities. They are typically expressed by employees as "I haven't been keeping up with some of the new developments in my field," "I can't get along with many of my coworkers," or "I can't use the new CAD system."

The "won't do's" reflect a lack of job motivation or interest. They are expressed as "My job is no longer challenging to me," "I'm no longer working on interesting projects," "I'm not being paid enough for what I'm expected to accomplish," or "I'm tired of doing the same things over and over again."

The "don't know what to do's" represent feelings of job ambiguity, often resulting in high levels of stress. These feelings are normally expressed by such statements as "I don't understand what my boss expects of me," "I have no idea how good a job I'm doing," or "I don't know where the company is going or my part in it."

When you find that there is a gap in your employee's performance, don't wait to deal with it. The problem will not go away; it will only become bigger and take up even more of your time. Start off by asking the employee if the performance gap could be caused by any of the factors outside of the organization and thoroughly investigate the various outside factors. Then move on to discussing factors inside the organization that could be causing the performance gap. Cover all four areas of performance blocks with the employee in the same fashion. Since the performance problem can be caused by more than one of the four factors, the diagnostic process should not stop simply because one factor has been identified. Only after all the various causes of the performance problem have been identified can you begin thinking about ways of closing the gap through action plans.

By using this performance diagnosis strategy, Terry helped Pat identify herself as the cause of the gap. She realized that she spent a great deal of her time recruiting and selecting new employees, making it impossible to give her reps four hours a week.

Phase 3: Develop Action Plans. Once you have identified the causes of your employee's gap, you need to determine the steps that will close that gap and enhance performance. Let's assume that you and one of your employees have met and decided that the performance problem is caused by you *and* by the employee. When you are the cause of the gap, you will need to change your behavior in some way. For example, you may need to communicate changes in company policies more frequently, or to communicate the division's business plans more effectively.

If the employee is also the cause of the gap, he or she may need to do the job differently, rethink priorities, or seek additional training. For example, you and the employee might realize that he needs to participate in a training program on improving customer service. It is important that these plans be specific: exactly what training program will he attend, when, and how will he use what he learns to close the gap?

Terry and Pat have decided that to eliminate Pat's performance gap, she will follow this four-part action plan:

1.   Pat will delegate part of the responsibility of recruiting and selecting new employees to two of her senior customer service reps, Joe Ferguson and Cathy Stewart.
2.   She will provide them with training in recruiting and selecting by February 15.

3.   Starting February 15, Pat will average at least four hours
     per week working with her reps.
4.   She will devote one of the four hours to gathering informa-
     tion concerning customer complaints and report this infor-
     mation to Terry the 1st and 15th of each month.

Phase 4: Provide Feedback. The final phase of the cycle
is designed to ensure that employees are given ongoing feedback and support for their improvement efforts. Very few employees can maintain high levels of motivation without feedback.
Make sure your employees know how they are doing in their
efforts to meet agreed-upon action plans, as well as other aspects
of their performance.

To ensure that the feedback you give to an employee is
appropriate, ask yourself if it meets the following criteria:

- Does the feedback fit the employee? Will it be meaningful
  enough to help the employee improve? Is the feedback appropriate, in the sense that the employee feels he or she
  deserves it? Is the feedback something the employee values?
- Is the focus of the feedback specific enough? Is it directly
  related to employee job performance? What did the employee
  specifically do that deserves feedback? How does it help the
  employee, the department, and the organization?
- Is the timing of the feedback right? Is it given soon after
  the behavior occurs? The closer to the behavior the feedback occurs, the more impact it will have on future performance.

The more the feedback fits the person involved, focuses on specific job performance, and occurs soon enough after the behavior,
the greater the effect on your employee's performance.

Managers with suddenly larger spans of control can easily feel overworked. The solutions provided here will make your
job easier in the long run and help your employees so they will
not have to be working scared.

MANAGERIAL SUCCESS POINTERS
Achieving Success with a Larger Span of Control

➤ Seek out aspects of your job that can be delegated.

➤ Support the three success strategies for employees.

➤ Identify gaps between current and expected job performance.

➤ Discover which performance blocks are influencing performance.

➤ Identify ways to close the gap.

➤ Provide feedback that fits the employee, occurs soon after the behavior, and focuses on specific job performance.

Two

Collaborating in
a Team Culture

The increased use of teams is one of the most important trends in American business today. Teams are used at all hierarchical levels, from the factory floor to "mahogany row," for one simple reason — the expectation of improving productivity and quality.

Let's look at a few specific illustrations of how teams have improved productivity:

- Through team direction, as well as flexible automation and computerized systems, productivity was increased by 250 percent at the General Electric plant in Salisbury, North Carolina.[1]
- Xerox plants using work teams report 30 percent greater productivity than their conventionally organized plants.[2]
- Procter & Gamble has reported 20 to 40 percent higher levels of productivity at its eighteen team-based plants.[3]
- General Motors Corporation reports a 20 to 40 percent increase in productivity in its team-based manufacturing plants.[4]
- Federal Express cut service glitches such as lost packages and billing errors by 13 percent as a result of teams.[5]
- A handful of large U.S. companies, such as Chrysler Corporation, have instituted corporate venture teams that can create new products quickly and successfully. These teams, made up of ten to fifteen people from many corporate areas, function as an autonomous small business and are able to bypass the usual corporate bureaucracy and red tape.[6]

- Honeywell's use of teams in the industrial automation systems division reduced cycle times by 30 percent; the teams were able to ship 99.6 percent of orders on time and generate $11.1 million in cost savings.[7]
- Since team direction was instituted in 1987 at the Morrisville repair facility of Northern Telecom, revenue has increased 63 percent, sales by 26 percent, and earnings by 46 percent. Moreover, productivity per employee has increased by more than 60 percent, scrap is down 63 percent, and quality has risen 50 percent.[8]
- Shenandoah Life Insurance Company reports that it is able to process 50 percent more applications and customer service requests, with 10 percent fewer people, now that employees are organized into teams.[9]

When we talk about teams in this book, we mean any group of employees who come together to channel their energies toward achieving a common purpose, something that none of them could possibly accomplish alone. There are many different types of teams — management teams, self-directed work teams composed of hourly employees, new venture teams, quality circles, task forces, and new products teams — but the best ones have one thing in common: synergism. Synergism has been defined as "the simultaneous actions of separate entities which together have greater total effect than the sum of their individual effects."[10]

In this chapter, you will learn some of the things that employees and managers can do to create high-producing teams with the electric, exhilarating energy we call synergism.

Mike's Story

Mike Martens is the maintenance manager at a large Illinois plant that manufactures aluminum foil. He started with the company fifteen years ago, right after college, and has been in charge of all mechanical and electrical maintenance activities at the plant for the past five years. As maintenance manager, Mike has eight first-line shift supervisors and one hundred maintenance employees under his direction.

Here's how Mike describes himself: "I had been raised as a Theory X manager. The management style I learned was, I direct, you follow, or you leave. I did this with great efficiency. I treated people fairly, but I also treated them like machines, not people."

Several weeks ago, Mike and other managers at the plant received a directive from the corporate staff, calling for a move from a traditional hierarchical environment to what they called a "team-based, employee involvement culture." Mike was not totally clear what this "team stuff" would mean for him, but he immediately felt that he wasn't going to like it.

In the past, Mike handled all decisions about hiring, planning, scheduling, and budgeting within his department. This is what he is accustomed to and this is the way he feels comfortable. Now, according to Mike, "All these traditional ideas are going out the window, since I'm expected to somehow get my first-line supervisors involved in a maintenance team."

This is not the only change caused by the team concept. Mike has heard that he will be a member of a plant operations team, consisting of the plant manager (Nancy Epson) and the managers of production, quality assurance, safety and health, and human resources. Mike is worried that this operations team is going to mean that he's no longer going to be "calling all the shots" in the maintenance department. He is not interested in "poking his nose" in other managers' operations. Besides, Mike does not get along with Glenn Long, the production manager, and doesn't like the prospect of working with him.

Mike wants to continue to achieve success with the company. He has always enjoyed managing the maintenance function, and he likes Nancy Epson. But now he's working scared.

Strategies for Employees

Mike is scared because he doesn't really know what teams are all about, and he doesn't know what it takes to succeed at being a team member. There are things he could do—you too, if you find yourself in a similar situation.

Assess Your Team-Player Style

There are four different types of team players:[11]

1. *Contributors.* These task-oriented team members see their main role as providing information; they willingly offer all the relevant knowledge, skills, data, and opinions that they possess. Often, contributors function as trainers and mentors of other team members. Being task-oriented, they're good at helping their team establish high standards, clarify priorities, and make effective use of time and resources.

2. *Collaborators.* These goal-directed team members remind the team to stay on track and focused on the steps necessary to reach the target. They will gladly work outside their defined roles to help out other team members; you'll never hear them say, "That's not my job." They work hard to achieve team goals even though they may not agree with them. Collaborators are open to new ideas and data even when the information alters the team's goals or plans. Their openness extends to constructive response to negative feedback.

3. *Communicators.* These process-oriented team members give their primary attention to helping the team through the process of accomplishing its goals. They step in to resolve conflict, recognize other members' efforts, and encourage others to participate in discussions and decision making. They provide constructive feedback, listen attentively to all viewpoints, communicate enthusiasm about the team's work, and help team members get to know one another and the skills and resources each can offer.

4. *Challengers.* These team members play the important role of devil's advocate. If they believe it will help the team, they question goals, methods, and perhaps even ethics. They speak out even when their views might be contrary to the other team members, even if it means being viewed by others as poor team players.

Which type are you? The truth is, it makes no difference; all four are equally important, all are needed for any high-performance team. The best teams have a healthy mix of members who focus on tasks, goals, process, and questioning. In fact, the most effective team members are a combination of types. They may have a natural leaning toward one style, but they have the capacity to call on the strengths of other styles when needed for the benefit of the team.

Mike has given a great deal of thought to this question of style. He sees himself as a contributor with high levels of technical knowledge and experience in the maintenance area. He has always been willing to share his expertise with others, and he takes pride in the mentoring he has given to maintenance employees in the past. These are excellent qualities, but for team participation Mike needs to begin working on developing his capacities as a collaborator, communicator, and challenger.

Understand How Teams Develop

Teams, much like people, go through definite stages of growth. You will be a better team player if you understand the stages. The four stages of team development are:[12]

1. Forming
2. Storming
3. Norming
4. Performing

During the forming stage, you and other team members will have to be flexible, for there is a great deal of role ambiguity. After all, you're not sure what types of behaviors are acceptable, what your team leader and members are like, what your team is expected to accomplish, and what processes are supposed to follow in achieving its mission. In this first stage, you could take a wait-and-see attitude, but then you'd probably be working scared. There is a better way: instead of sitting still, get involved. You could:[13]

- Ask your manager for his or her view of the team's purposes, procedures, and norms.
- Work on getting to know your fellow team members.
- Offer your services to help your team get things clarified.
- Tactfully express questions or reservations you may have about the team's purpose or methods.

Mike finds himself in the *forming* stage. Rather than sitting by and doing nothing, he has decided to meet with Nancy to find out all he can about what the introduction of teams is going to mean for the plant and for himself. During their talk, Mike is going to express to Nancy all of his current concerns about this large change in organizational culture.

The *storming* stage is a period of antagonism among team members, hostility toward the team leader, and resistance toward the team's task. Try to keep in mind that this stage is normal, and that it will eventually pass. You can also help by encouraging your fellow team members to express their hostility openly, keeping an open mind to what others are saying, stating your own concerns, and suggesting ways to resolve differences.

The *norming* stage is the time the team settles in and gets down to work. Processes are ironed out, and the group's particular ways of working — the norms — are gradually developed. Be careful that you and your team don't slide into "groupthink" — when everyone starts to think alike. It creates a climate that inhibits team members from willingly challenging the prevailing thinking. If allowed to persist, groupthink will inhibit innovativeness and problem solving. Tackle groupthink by asking your fellow team members, "Are we smoothing over basic disagreements?"[14]

In the *performing* stage, your team is sailing along, truly functioning as a team. Unfortunately, sometimes team members get complacent or bored now that all is running smoothly, slip back into bad habits, or fail to keep up to date with new technology. You can help your team cope with all this by recommending new and challenging task assignments, facilitating team meetings aimed at discovering new directions for your team, encouraging exhilarating celebrations involving all team members, and confronting your team with the signs of stagnation you see.[15]

Be Ready for New Responsibilities

Working in teams is much more than just a way to get tasks accomplished; it also brings changes to the individuals who make up the team. They learn new skills, perhaps work in different areas, and assume more responsibility. These are three of the main ways that teams have the effect of empowering people.

You hear a lot about "empowerment" these days. What exactly does it mean? The authors of a recent book entitled *Empowered Teams* do an excellent job of explaining the term. "Power means 'control, authority, dominion.' The prefix *em* means 'to put on to' or 'to cover with.' Empowering, then, is passing on authority and responsibility. As we refer to it here, empowerment occurs when power goes to employees who then experience a sense of ownership and control over their jobs. Empowered individuals know that their jobs belong to them. Given a say in how things are done, employees feel more responsible. When they feel more responsible, they show more initiative in their work, get more done, and enjoy the work more."[16]

Learning New Skills. Often in team environments, members are expected to learn, over time, some or all of the tasks on their team. Multiskilling, as it is called, is used with both white-collar and blue-collar jobs. For instance, at the Weyerhaeuser plant in Columbus, Mississippi, operating technicians are encouraged, but not required, to learn all their team's tasks, which can involve up to twelve years of training.

To become a valuable part of the plant operations team, Mike is going to have to broaden himself. Although he's an excellent contributor in the maintenance function, he will have to begin learning more about the other managerial functions. It's not going to be easy to learn new things, but Mike will be better off in the end, particularly since his long-range career aspiration is to become a plant manager.

Rotating Jobs. Once team members learn new skills, they can expect to be rotated from task to task. For instance, at the Logan Aluminum plant in Russellville, Kentucky, team members participate in what is called the star point system, named for the five points of a star. Five primary star point representatives (for the areas of quality, safety, operations, human resources, and resource adviser) and corresponding alternates are selected from within the work group. The primary representatives serve for six months, then rotate out, replaced by the alternates. Star point representatives who have completed their assignments either rotate back into the team or assume another star point role (either primary or alternate) within the team. The rotation process gives all team members the opportunity to participate in the day-to-day management of work group activities.[17]

At some point, the star point system will be used in Mike's plant operation team. When this occurs, he is going to be expected to participate as a star point representative. This will involve rotating, every four months, through the five points of the star — administration, production, quality assurance, safety and health, and human resources.

Assuming More Responsibility. As team members approach higher levels of empowerment, they take on more of the responsibilities normally reserved for management. Shown below are just a few traditional managerial responsibilities that team members may undertake:

Purchasing equipment	Scheduling production
Hiring team members	Training each other
Taking disciplinary action	Scheduling vacations
Budgeting	Appraising performance
Making pay decisions	Contacting customers
Being responsible for quality	Designing facilities
Handling personnel issues	Housekeeping
Cross-functional teaming	Managing suppliers
Conducting meetings	Planning

Here are a few concrete examples of added responsibility in action:

- At Lake Superior Paper Industries, team members handle their own work scheduling and work assignments, as well as holiday and vacation planning. [18]
- At the Volvo plant in Uddevalla, Sweden, self-directed work teams assemble entire cars. [19]
- At Johnsonville Food, a sausage company in Wisconsin, teams not only schedule their own work and uphold quality standards but also decide whether it's advisable to take certain large orders. [20]
- At Chrysler, platform teams consisting of about a thousand people have cross-functional representation (design, manufacturing, marketing, distribution) from throughout the company. Each team is responsible for putting a vehicle on the road on time, at cost, and in the correct weight classification. [21]

Work on Keeping Communications Open

What do you do when you begin to dislike or distrust a fellow team member? If you're like most of us, you do whatever you can to avoid that person. Whenever team members stop communicating, team performance will inevitably suffer. A whole host of negative consequences can occur:

- Witholding needed information
- Sabotaging
- Confusion
- Stress
- Frustration
- Resistance to bringing up problems
- Reluctance to offering solutions to problems

Clearly, open communication is critical to any high-performance team. The more frequently and openly team members communicate with one another, the more likely they will perform well.

Let's talk about the specific things that you should do, as a team member, to facilitate open communications between others and yourself.

Convey Equality and Mutual Respect. It's very unlikely that everybody on your team possesses the same level of talent, experience, ability, power, or status. In fact, you might be one of the more talented or powerful members of your team. If so, you have to be especially careful of your tone of voice and your mannerisms. Convey superiority, and you'll stifle openness. Beware of saying things like this:

> "I've been around here long enough to know that it won't work."
> "If you had listened to what I told you before, we wouldn't be having all these problems."
> "After you get as experienced as I am, you'll understand what I mean."

What you need to do is to treat team members in a way that subtly says:

> "I respect your ideas."
> "I'm listening, even though I see things differently."
> "I value your opinion."
> "We're all in this together."

Avoid Putdowns. When people are put down, made to feel foolish, or degraded, they react in one of two ways: they withdraw or they retaliate. In either case, team performance suffers.

Effective team members are not content with the status quo. They're always looking for new ways to improve equipment, people, and methods. To do this, they have to be willing to generate new ideas, even if some of them turn out wrong. Team members cannot be improvement-minded if they are always looking over their shoulders worrying about being put down by others.

Here are three very common — and very destructive — kinds of putdowns. As you read them, ask yourself whether you do any of these things when participating on a team.

- *Sweeping statements.* Using the terms "always" or "never" when discussing a team member's job performance can be a major putdown. Telling people that they are *"always* late for team meetings" or *"never* willing to pitch in" will inevitably make them angry and defensive. You'll be doing much better by simply saying: "Jane, I've noticed that sometimes you've been showing up late for team meetings" or "Tom, how about giving us a hand?" Stay far away from sweeping statements, even if they are accurate.

- *Personal attacks.* When disagreeing with a fellow team member, focus on the issue, not the person. Personal attacks — such things as "you're dead wrong," "you don't know what you're talking about," "you've missed the point," "you're being foolish," "you're naive if you can believe that," and "if you'd listen better, you'd understand what I mean" — are destructive because they belittle the other person's self-esteem. Instead, you need to keep your disagreements centered on the issue. Use statements such as "here's where I think we disagree," "as I see it," and "here's what I think the main point is."

- *Gotcha!* The game of "I gotcha" is deadly in a team environment. When team members are told things such as "I told you so" and "See, I was right all along," it isn't long before they stop contributing altogether.

Learn to Listen. Listening goes beyond merely hearing. It also involves being open-minded, being willing to at least seriously consider other people's viewpoints.

Good team players show more interest in the success of their team than in being proved "right." They're willing to listen to opposing viewpoints, if the ideas are in the best interest of their team.

Show Empathy. Team members stop communicating with others on their team who act as though their feelings and welfare are not important. The opposite of this attitude is empathy.

What can you say to show your fellow team members that you share their concerns? Here are a few suggestions:

"I understand how you feel."
"I'd feel the same way if I were in your position."
"What can I do to help you out?"

Mike realizes that he needs to improve his relationship with Glenn Long if the two of them are going to be valuable contributors to the plant operations team. Mike sees that he needs to stop playing the game of "I gotcha" with Glenn and start doing a better job of really listening to his point of view.

Dealing with Ineffective Team Players

Although the team leader is critical to the success of the team, the leader cannot be responsible for solving all problems. Team members must share in the responsibility for leadership. This is extremely important in dealing with team players who are ineffective.

A few years ago we were working with team leaders and technicians in a large pulp and paper mill in Mississippi. The mill, which had just recently started operation, had self-directed work teams. During one of our visits, we heard that one of the teams was having difficulty training some of the new technicians. Apparently, two senior-level male technicians on the paper machine were resisting the training of newly hired female technicians. In fact, they were barely talking to the trainees.

In a traditional operation, the shift supervisor would have a long talk with the two senior technicians, in the hope of getting them to be more cooperative. Not so in this team culture. Here, a few members of the team stopped work, met for about a half hour with the two senior technicians in the team's meeting room, and solved the problem among themselves, with no assistance needed from either their team leader or representatives from the human resources department.

Fortunately, this success story is not an unusual incident within high-performing teams. Team members who observe counterproductive team players are able to handle these situations. They don't have to wait for supervisors to solve problems for them.

Here are some specific ways for dealing with ineffective team members:[22]

- *Meet in private.* Nobody wants to be embarrassed by being criticized publicly. Meet with the team member either privately or in a small-group setting.
- *Confront.* Explain the behaviors the person is exhibiting that are hurting your team's performance, and why. Don't describe the problem in terms of personal traits such as "you're uncooperative" or "you are selfish." Instead, point out specific actions that are inhibiting your team.
- *Actively listen.* Give your fellow team member an opportunity to state his side of the issue. He may have a legitimate reason for his actions, or you may be misinterpreting his behavior.
- *Revisit team norms.* Every team has its own set of norms, accepted ways of doing things that all are expected to follow. These norms pertain to a whole range of behaviors such as attendance and participation in meetings, adherence to safety rules, training others, continued growth and learning, punctuality, and attendance. Remind the team member of those expected behaviors that she is not performing.
- *Create positive consequences.* Social pressure from the rest of the team will typically be enough to bring about an immediate improvement in the team member's job performance. However, it isn't usually enough to sustain a lasting behavioral change. To accomplish this, your team will need to create positive consequences for doing the desired behavior. Depending on the individual team member, these positive consequences might be such things as receiving recognition, getting the team's okay to learn new tasks, working with newer

---

EMPLOYEE SUCCESS POINTERS
Achieving Success in a Team Culture

➤ Improve your own primary team style.

➤ Work on increasing your other styles.

➤ Recognize and learn to adapt to the four stages of team development as they occur.

➤ Be ready for the three types of empowerment you will experience as a team member.

➤ Use techniques to facilitate open communications between other team members and yourself.

➤ Know how to deal with team members who are being ineffective.

---

equipment, having more flexible work hours, getting the opportunity to travel to other locations, having direct contact with customers, and performing choice assignments.

Strategies for Managers

Even in the best circumstances, people who are assigned to work teams will be uncertain at first. The natural tendency is to look toward their managers for guidance. What can managers do to help make teams successful?

Check for Feasibility

To begin with, managers need to realize that not all organizations will be receptive to the team concept. Management should commission a feasibility study to explore the organization's readiness for self-directed teams. A steering committee consisting of a diverse group of influential people, including managers, staff people, hourly employees, and union leaders, should be assembled. The steering committee should visit other organizations that are already using self-directed teams, to see for themselves how teams function. The authors of *Self-Directed Work Teams* recommend that the steering committee use interviews and questionnaires to get detailed answers to these six crucial questions:[23]

1. Are the work processes compatible with self-directed work teams?
2. Are employees willing and able to make self-direction work?
3. Can managers master and apply the hands-off leadership style required by self-directed teams?
4. Is the market healthy or promising enough to support improved productivity without reducing the work force?
5. Will the organization's policies and culture in both corporate and field locations support the transition to teams?
6. Will the community support the transition to teams?

A steering committee has been in existence at Mike's plant for the past twelve months. Committee members have visited several other metals plants that have implemented a team culture and were impressed with the results. They have also conducted a feasibility study by interviewing a representative sample of plant employees. After gathering all their data, they analyzed and concluded that all six crucial questions could be answered affirmatively.

Deal with Your Own Fears

It's important to remember that not all managers are alike. Some will welcome the transition to a self-managed work force as a needed change; most will experience fear and anxiety. The simple truth is that managers face even more severe changes than do team members. In the past, a manager's role has traditionally been to plan, control, and direct. Managers in conventional organizations told their employees what to do, when to do it, and how. They spent a lot of time carefully overseeing their employees' work as well as fighting daily fires. Now, as organizations begin implementing teams, managers have to help their employees find their *own* solutions to problems. This is difficult for most traditional managers to handle. They are afraid that they will become unnecessary and obsolete.

Let's listen to Mike's fears: "Turning over all the things that I had been successful in managing to my first-line supervisors, who had never been trained in these areas, is scary. Besides, if I can't be a success in this team environment, I could lose my position and jeopardize my career and all the things I've worked for over the years. I'm also worried that we're going to risk our plant's success by turning over the asylum to the inmates."

What should managers like Mike do to cope with this difficult transition?

Attend Manager Awareness Sessions. Most companies moving to work teams institute some type of awareness sessions to educate their managers about the transition. These sessions are intended to help managers see that giving up some of their long-time duties also has its benefits. The managers come to realize that the extra time that they gained as a result of the team's self-management allows them to take care of other important matters such as long-term planning and customer service that they have had to keep on the back burner.

Update Management Skills. Awareness training sessions by themselves will not be enough to alleviate managers' fears. Managers need to update their supervisory skills, as well as learn new ones.

To achieve success in a team culture, managers must perfect these critical skills:[24]

1. Build trust within their teams, as well as between their teams and themselves.
2. Work with their teams to clarify performance expectations and criteria.
3. Foster commitment and trust among team members.
4. Decide when it is appropriate to lead and not to lead.
5. Recognize their team's accomplishments.
6. Coach new team members in mastering their roles within the team.

7. Encourage their teams to find additional ways to self-manage.
8. Work collaboratively with teams when expectations are not being achieved.
9. Facilitate team meetings.
10. Solve problems in cooperation within their teams.

Use a Hand-Off Plan. A hand-off plan is a process for deciding which tasks in the work unit are going to be handed off to the team and which will be retained by management.[25] The process has several steps. First, all team members and managers keep, for one week, a personal log of all the tasks that make up their day. Next, everyone on the team meets together to develop a complete list of tasks required to get the team's work accomplished. Another team meeting is then held to put all tasks in one of these six categories:

1. The task should become an immediate team member responsibility.
2. The task should eventually become a team member responsibility.
3. The task should become the responsibility of the team leader.
4. The task should remain or become a management responsibility.
5. A formal procedure should be developed to handle this task.
6. The task is not necessary; nobody on the team needs to perform it.

Mike and his eight first-line supervisors met as a team. With the help of a facilitator from the human resources department, they used the hand-off plan to clarify "who's going to do what." This process of role clarification has made Mike feel a lot more comfortable delegating responsibility and authority downward.

Recognize That Teams Are Not a Panacea

Although organizing employees into teams has enormous potential for increasing productivity, managers should *never* regard teams as a cure-all for personnel or productivity problems. Like most other type of organizational interventions, teams can be a source of headaches that managers should be ready to deal with. Let's look at a few of these headaches.

First, no matter how professionally and carefully teams are introduced into an organization, there will always be some managers who won't be able to make the transition. For instance, at Northern Telecom, about 25 percent of first-line supervisors left after team direction was implemented.[26]

Second, sometimes work teams fail. Unfortunately, teamwork doesn't occur naturally in our country's culture. In general, Americans have been conditioned since childhood to be competitive rather than cooperative. American workers have to unlearn their natural tendencies to be individualistic (concerned with "I") rather than collectivistic (concerned with "we"). This change is particularly difficult when employees perceive a lack of senior management support for the transition to teams.

Third, managers have to realize that they must be patient. The road to team self-direction is long and rocky. Jim Meyer, director of operations at Schott Transformers, warns, "Things won't be neat and tidy. Expect chaos at first. It's also wise to move with caution."[27] How long should it take before managers see steady results? According to our experiences, about two years.

Facilitate Problem Solving

One of the most important functions that managers perform is to help their teams solve work-related problems. Before, during, and after these problem-solving meetings, the manager's actions are critical.

Beforehand, managers need to formulate a kick-off question that will be posed at the beginning of the meeting. This kick-off question had better be right on target, since it establishes the direction for the entire meeting. If it's off target, the meeting will turn out to be a waste of time, as many meetings are. This kick-off question also has to be posed in such a way as to stimulate team discussion.

To accomplish the objectives, managers must first give

some thought to the real purpose of their team meeting. Is the team getting together to pinpoint the causes of existing problems, or to find solutions?

Suppose, for example, the team is getting together to discuss problems of providing more courteous service to surgical patients in a large city hospital. If the manager believes that the causes of the problems have not been discussed and agreed on by the team, then the kick-off question might be "What things do you believe are causing us to have difficulty providing quality service to our surgical patients?" On the other hand, if the manager feels that the causes of the problems are known, then the kick-off question might be "What do we need to do to improve service to our patients?"

During the meeting, the manager should take the role of team facilitator. This involves:

- Explaining the purpose of the meeting by posing the kick-off question to the team.
- Keeping the meetings orderly and focused on the kick-off question.
- Ensuring that every team member has an opportunity to talk, "tell it like it is," and be heard.
- Summarizing the results or major issues addressed.
- Making sure that every team member leaves a problem-solving session understanding what needs to be done, who will do it, and when it will be accomplished.

After a problem-solving meeting, at agreed-upon checkpoints, the manager should touch base with each of the team members to learn how things are progressing and to find out if they might need some help. It's a good idea, too, to call a follow-up meeting to celebrate the team's accomplishments.

At first, Mike found it extremely difficult to use this problem-solving technique. As a traditional manager, he wasn't used to having his staff participate in identifying the causes of problems or solving them. That was *his* job! Now Mike is beginning to learn, more and more each day, that the quality of solutions to maintenance problems can be found and implemented better with his team's input.

Foster Teamwork

By far the most important function of any manager in a team environment is to foster teamwork. Without real teamwork, a team will experience communication problems, backbiting, sabotage, job dissatisfaction, griping, low morale, and interpersonal conflicts.

Here are some valuable tips that managers should follow for promoting teamwork:

• *Hold an annual retreat.* Schedule an annual retreat for the whole team to build team spirit, talk about the team's vision and goals, renew commitment to the team, and get to know one another better. In some cases, it is advisable to ask an organization development consultant skilled in team building to function as a facilitator at the retreat.

• *Assess decision-making style.* Managers need to assess their own decision-making style. They need to pay particular attention to the extent to which they solicit their team members' ideas before arriving at important decisions. They need to make sure they are not still making decisions unilaterally. They need to find opportunities for using a consensus method — which, by the way, usually results in better outcomes.

Changing his decision-making style has not been easy for Mike. At first, he went 180 degrees in the opposite direction. He changed totally from being a control-oriented manager to a hands-off one. He thought that this was the way teams were supposed to be managed. Like others, he confused participative management with no management. With time, Mike is getting better at using a consensus decision-making approach.

• *Draw out quiet team members.* Managers need to find ways to involve quiet team members in group discussions and decision making, and do so in a way that doesn't embarrass them. The use of open-ended questions and reflective listening often helps.

- *Agree that it's OK to disagree.* The norm of "we are willing to allow disagreement" is an important ingredient for all teams. Without it, groupthink occurs. Managers themselves are the most powerful motivators of healthy disagreement. They need to demonstrate that it is not only permissible but valuable for team members to voice disagreement with them and with one another.

- *Celebrate team accomplishments.* Managers need to find ways to reward team accomplishments, celebrate the team, and share success with team members. They need to show appreciation to both line and administrative staff. All this boils down to what Tom Peters and Bob Waterman referred to as "hoopla" in their popular book, *In Search of Excellence.* [28]

- *Encourage trust.* Managers must foster an environment of trust among their team members, as well as between themselves and their teams. This is accomplished by ensuring that all criticisms are constructive, that everyone focuses on behaviors, not personalities. Managers need to make certain that they always level with their people and are never found distorting the truth. It's better, in the long run, to say things that the team might not like hearing, than to try to fool them.

- *Share the limelight.* When opportunities for external recognition occur, effective managers don't hog the limelight — they spread it around among team members. Whether it's accepting an award from the local community, making a presentation to upper-level management, participating on highly visible committees in the organization, or getting named in the company newspaper, effective managers make sure that everyone receives time in the limelight.

- *Clarify norms and expectations.* Effective managers work collaboratively with their team members on clarifying the team's norms so that everyone understands and agrees upon the standards of behavior. In this way, everyone understands what's expected of them. Nobody is working scared, worrying whether

---

MANAGERIAL SUCCESS POINTERS
Achieving Success in a Team Culture

➤ Conduct a feasibility study to explore whether your organization is really ready for moving to a team culture.

➤ Acknowledge any of your fears about teams and work on coping with them.

➤ Realize that, despite their advantages, teams can also be a source of headaches.

➤ Make certain that you know how to facilitate problem-solving meetings with your team.

➤ Arrange an annual retreat to foster teamwork.

➤ Assess your own decision-making style.

➤ Encourage trust among team members.

➤ Don't hog the limelight; share it with your team.

➤ Work collaboratively with your team to clarify norms and expectations.

➤ Initiate a semiannual or quarterly self-examination of how well your team is functioning.

---

other team members approve of what they're doing. Here are a few illustrations of norms:

> We attend all team meetings.
> We don't bad-mouth our team in the presence of outsiders.
> We show up for work ten to fifteen minutes early.
> We state our opinions even if they don't reflect the popular thing to say.

• *Take the team's temperature.* Teams, like people, need to have periodic checkups. Teams cannot afford to be complacent and just assume that everything is going great. Managers can help their teams by initiating a quarterly or semiannual self-examination where the team asks itself questions such as these:

> Have we been accomplishing our goals?
> Are we meeting our customers' needs?
> What can we do to function better as a team?
> Is everyone on the team clear as to what's expected of them?

Mike has surprised himself how well he has managed to adapt to the introduction of teams in the maintenance department. The success experienced by the maintenance team thus far has been due greatly to Mike's ability to clarify norms and expectations, celebrate team accomplishments, and update his managerial style.

THREE

Succeeding in a Quality-Focused Organization

TQM. SPC. TQC. Pareto charts. SQC. MDQ. Kaizen. Shewhart cycle. Histogram. QFD.

What do all these terms have in common? Quality. They are all related to the quality movement that is rapidly spreading throughout today's changing organizations. Spend enough time in the halls of any organization in the United States and you will hear one of those words. The corridors of corporate America are talking quality—if you are not, then you are probably working scared.

Total Quality Management

• You bought a new car last week. This morning you got in to go to work and your one-week-old car did not start. When you called your car dealer the reponse was, "No problem, we will take care of it; it happens all the time."

• Yesterday you had lunch at a trendy restaurant near work. You had to get back to work for an early-afternoon meeting. The waiter brought coffee, but you had to ask for cream three times. When he finally brought the cream, the waiter acted as though he had just done you a big favor.

• Recently, you got a letter from your insurance company stating that your automobile insurance was cancelled because you ignored your last statement. When you called the

45

company and said that you didn't receive a statement, the customer service representative replied that all statements were sent out on the first of the month. "Besides, it is spelled out clearly in your policy that it is your responsibility to know when premiums are due." A couple of weeks later you received a letter of apology from the insurance company. There had been a computer error, it turned out, and many of the statements had never been sent out!

These low levels of quality may have been acceptable in the past, but they will not be acceptable in the future. Customers will no longer be impressed to receive the product or service they ordered; they will consider it a prerequisite to doing business. Quality goods and services will likely become what quality guru Phil Crosby calls the "price of admission" to the future world economy.[1] Realizing the importance of quality to their future competitiveness, many organizations have implemented a new way of doing business, called Total Quality Management (TQM).

What Is TQM?

Although TQM is unique to each organization that uses the approach, the fundamental meaning is that it seeks to improve product quality and customer satisfaction through companywide practices. Some of the major premises of TQM include:

- *Continuous improvement and employee involvement.* Everyone in the organization, from the boardroom to the mailroom, searches for daily incremental improvements.
- *Empowerment.* Everyone is provided with the training and the techniques of quality improvement as well as the authority to identify and solve problems.
- *Demanding goals.* High quality performance targets are set and the results are continually analyzed and measured.
- *Strong customer-driven quality vision.* The strategic vision of the company is focused on the needs of the customer. Quality is defined by the customer. The organization strives to improve every product, service, and organizational process.

The Gurus of the Quality Movement

Because so many names come up in current discussions of quality, we mention some of the prominent individuals in the quality movement and summarize their contributions below.

Philip B. Crosby. Crosby was vice president for quality at ITT from 1965 to 1979. After writing a best-selling book entitled *Quality Is Free,* he resigned from ITT and went on the lecture circuit.[2] He started a consulting firm that provided training in quality at all levels, senior executives through hourly employees. That firm, which still bears his name although it has recently been sold, has 280 employees and has annual revenues of $84 million.[3]

Crosby believes that executives in many companies have been reinforced over the years to compromise everything in order to produce profit. He believes that profits are a function of customer satisfaction, that quality must be the result of a carefully planned and constructed culture and it must become the actual fabric of the organization. In his second book, *Quality Without Tears,* Crosby spelled out four quality absolutes (see Exhibit 3.1).[4]

Crosby expands on his four basic principles and has a fourteen-point program to implement quality throughout an organization. He believes these fourteen steps provide the foundation for a quality culture within an organization.

Crosby's Fourteen-Step Quality Improvement Process

1. Management commitment
2. Quality improvement team
3. Measurement
4. Cost of quality
5. Awareness
6. Corrective action
7. Zero defects planning
8. Employee education
9. Zero defects day
10. Goal setting

Exhibit 3.1. Crosby's Four Absolutes of Quality Management.

---

1. *"The definition of quality is conformance to requirements"* (p. 58). The requirements that employees are expected to meet must be established. They must then be given the skills, training, and help to meet those requirements. The idea behind quality is "getting everybody to do it right the first time" (p. 59).

2. *"The system for causing quality is prevention, not appraisal"* (p. 73). American industry has a tendency to check, inspect, or appraise problems *after* they have occurred. We should be concerned with preventing errors from occurring in the first place. The goal of American industry has apparently been to "make 1200 in order to have 900 that we could sell [while the Japanese] learned to make 1200 to have 1200 to sell" (p. 30). The Japanese have been more concerned with preventing the errors in the first place.

3. *"The performance standard must be zero defects, not 'that's close enough'"* (p. 84). Organizations continually reinforce errors in some areas and do not allow errors in others. For example, when it comes to payroll an organization and its employees typically expect zero defects. The payroll department is not necessarily more competent than other departments, it is just that they know people will not put up with errors in their paychecks. Yet employees on that company's production line are told that 2 percent defective parts is acceptable and customer service representatives are told 2 percent customer complaints is an adequate quality level. The only acceptable quality level should be zero defects.

4. *"The measurement of quality is the price of nonconformance"* (p. 85). The price of nonconformance is whatever it costs to do things wrong. If a product malfunctions and a customer must bring it back, there are costs involved. The work must be done over, the warranty must be paid for, the orders must be changed, paperwork has to be taken care of—this all adds up to an enormous cost. It could represent "20% or more of sales in manufacturing companies and 35% of operating costs in service companies" (pp. 85–86). By doing things right the first time, an organization can save an enormous amount.

Note: All quotations and page numbers in this exhibit are from P. B. Crosby, *Quality Is Free: The Art of Making Quality Certain* (New York: McGraw-Hill, 1979).

11. Error–cause removal
12. Recognition
13. Quality councils
14. Do it all again

W. Edwards Deming. Deming began consulting to Japanese companies on quality control methods in 1950. By 1951 the Japanese government established the Deming Prize for accomplishments in statistical theory and application. In 1960, Deming became the first American to be awarded the Second

Order of the Sacred Treasure for his help in the rebirth of Japanese industry. But for the next twenty years he remained virtually unknown in the United States. All that changed on June 24, 1980, with an NBC documentary entitled, "If Japan Can, Why Can't We?" The last quarter hour was devoted to Deming and his work. He immediately became sought after in the United States and began consulting to Ford and General Motors, among others. He has become the world's best-known quality guru. Deming's famous "Fourteen Points"[5] are highlighted and discussed in Exhibit 3.2.

Armand V. Feigenbaum. Feigenbaum joined General Electric as an engineer during World War II; very early on in his career he worked on the world's first jet engines. Because sometimes these engines worked and sometimes they did not, he used statistical techniques to find out what was going wrong and why. In the 1960s he was named manager of manufacturing operations for GE worldwide. He coined the term "total quality control" and in 1961 wrote a classic textbook in the area.[6] Feigenbaum stayed with GE until 1968 when he started General Systems Company, a consulting firm in Pittsfield, Massachusetts.

Feigenbaum's key ideas were summarized in a recent book entitled *Beyond Quality.* "His basic premise was that quality relates to every function and activity within the organization, not simply manufacturing and engineering but also traditional white-collar functions such as marketing and finance. Total Quality Control is defined as the system for integrating the quality development, quality maintenance, and quality improvement efforts of groups in an organization enabling production and service at the most economical levels which allow for full customer satisfaction."[7]

Feigenbaum believes that quality and costs are partners, and he argued early on that better quality does not cost more. In his view, quality is not just a way of managing or a generalized concept, but something that can be measured and quantified.

Kaoru Ishikawa. Ishikawa has been referred to as "the gurus' guru." Until his death in 1988, he was a university pro-

Exhibit 3.2. The Fourteen-Point Deming Management Method.

---

1. *"Create constancy of purpose for improvement of product and service."* Companies must look to the future and develop plans and methods that will allow them to stay in business. This must be done through innovation, research and education, continuous improvement of products and services, and maintenance of equipment and facilities.

2. *"Adopt the new philosophy."* The new religion of American industry must become QUALITY. Organizations must view poor workmanship and service as totally unacceptable.

3. *"Cease dependence on mass inspection."* It becomes too expensive to inspect products and then either rework them or throw them out. Rather, quality comes from improving the process so defects do not occur in the first place. Spend money improving the process rather than inspecting products.

4. *"End the practice of rewarding business on the price tag alone."* If the lowest-priced vendor is always chosen, this will frequently lead to low-quality supplies. Rather than jumping from vendor to vendor, it is better to seek the best quality and develop long-term relationships with a few or a single supplier.

5. *"Improve constantly and forever the system of production and service."* Everyone in every department in the company must continually look for ways to improve quality and reduce waste. Improvement cannot be looked at as a one-time effort but a continuous process.

6. *"Institute training."* Often workers learn about their jobs from other workers who were not trained properly to begin with. Workers often do not even know if they have done their jobs correctly. People must be provided with enough formal training. Whenever new equipment or processes are introduced, there must be new training as well.

7. *"Institute leadership."* Many times supervisors are hired straight out of college, have never done the jobs that they are supervising, and therefore are not very much help to the workers. That makes it too easy for a supervisor to rely on setting numbers and quotas and simply pushing for more productivity. Turning out products quickly becomes the norm, and quality is ignored. That is not leadership. Leading consists of coaching, giving feedback in a positive manner, and helping employees to do a better job.

8. *"Drive out fear."* To assure better quality and productivity, workers must feel secure enough to take a stand, ask questions when they do not understand, and point out problems without fear of being blamed for the problem. Fear must be driven out so employees can feel free to speak up.

9. *"Break down barriers between staff areas."* Often sales and marketing, manufacturing, engineering, purchasing, and customer service within one organization operate as if they are five different companies in competition with one another. Employees within each department can be doing exceptional jobs, surpassing what is expected of them, yet if the departmental goals are in conflict with the overall mission, they can ruin the company. There must be teamwork so employees are working for the common good of the company rather than only their individual departments.

10. *"Eliminate slogans, exhortations, and targets for the work force."* A slogan, no matter how imaginative, has never helped employees do a better job. If employees

Exhibit 3.2. The Fourteen-Point Deming Management Method, Cont'd.

---

put up a slogan, it ought to be their own slogan. Announcing bottom-line or results-oriented goals will not be effective unless the method or process for accomplishing these goals is also described.

11. *"Eliminate numerical quotas."* It is often communicated to workers that a quota must be reached at all costs. These "costs" often become lost customers, employee dissatisfaction, turnover, and poor quality. An organization is often damaged by strict adherence to numerical quotas because they take into account only numbers, not quality and methods.

12. *"Remove barriers to pride of workmanship."* If we are serious about quality, we must empower workers with the responsibility to make sure quality happens. Poorly informed managers, inferior materials, and defective equipment are all barriers that must be removed.

13. *"Institute a vigorous program of education and retraining."* An investment in the people that work in the organization is necessary for long-term success. Education in the new methods, including statistical techniques and teamwork, is required for managers and employees alike. Everybody in the entire organization should be given the education and help to improve.

14. *"Take action to accomplish the transformation."* To carry out the preceding thirteen points, a top-management team must be formed to carry out the quality mission. The transformation must occur around teamwork, use of statistical methods, thinking of work as satisfying a customer, and the continual improvement of methods and procedures.

Note: The quotations in this exhibit are in pp. 17–19 of M. Walton, *Deming's Management at Work* (New York: Putnam's, 1990).

fessor who lived most of his life in Tokyo. He invented quality circles back in 1962 and was in the forefront of Japan's quality revolution from the very beginning. Because Ishikawa was born into an aristocratic Japanese family, he was able to get the ear of Japan's most important leaders right from the start of his career. Some of his basic ideas include:

- Quality should be first, ahead of short-term profits.
- Organizations should have a consumer orientation, not a producer orientation.
- Commit to continuous improvement throughout the entire organization; quality touches every function within an organization and is everyone's job.
- Strip down work processes to eliminate problems that prevent quality, not to assign blame.

- Identify customers, internal and external, and satisfy their requirements.
- The reason for the existence of quality control is to design and develop products and services that are always useful and satisfactory to the consumer. (It is interesting to note that Ishikawa was putting the emphasis on the consumer in the 1950s; only recently have American executives attached importance to the relationship between quality and customers.)
- Provide all employees with the tools to use facts and data in making presentations and solving problems.
- There should be respect for humanity in management philosophy; instill pride in performance and encourage teamwork.

Joseph M. Juran. Like Deming, Juran is an American who had a tremendous influence in Japan long before he was well known in the United States. Juran's respected textbook, *Quality Control Handbook,* was published in 1951; shortly thereafter he began lecturing in Japan.[8] Some of his basic ideas include:

- Managing for quality control is similar to managing for financial control.
- Quality is a lot more than statistical tools; it involves identifying the customers and their needs, and designing goods and services to meet these needs.
- There should be a "project approach" to quality improvement, which includes the use of pareto analysis, a technique to target the key improvement opportunities.

The Juran "quality trilogy" became the cornerstone of thinking about quality:

Juran Quality Trilogy

1. Quality planning
2. Quality control
3. Quality improvement

Juran believes that quality programs often fail because managers at the top did not realize that achieving quality would be difficult. Top-level managers must be part of quality councils that guide and coordinate the process. They must also participate through accepting training, personally reviewing progress, and making it part of the reward system.

In 1989, Juran stepped down as head of the Juran Institute and passed the baton to A. Blanton Godfrey, former head of quality theory at Bell Labs. Godfrey believes that recent events show that Western executives must change their management styles. Not long ago these executives blamed their market problems on unfair competition, lazy workers, or inflated wages. "Then," Godfrey points out, "the Japanese opened factories in the U.S. and these slovenly, overpaid workers produced quality products."[9]

Taiichi Ohno. Ohno is vice president of Toyota Motor Company. Working with industrial engineering consultant Shigeo Shingo, he has designed and refined one of the most impressive production systems in the world. Ohno is credited with the idea of just-in-time, which the book *Beyond Quality* defines this way: "The concept of Just-in-Time (JIT) is simple but powerful: materials and components should arrive at the factory, or from one work station to another within a plant, at precisely the moment they are needed for use. No sooner, no later."[10]

For the JIT system to be effective, it requires "consistently high quality up and down the supply chain."[11] Organizations must be concerned not only with internal quality issues, but the quality methods used by their suppliers as well. The JIT method has become the model for manufacturing all over the world, including at plants of Black & Decker, Chrysler, Ford, GM, Motorola, Hewlett-Packard, 3M, and Johnson & Johnson.

Quality Awards

Two well-known awards have been established to honor achievements in quality, the Deming Prize and the Baldrige Award. Many organizations find that striving to win these prestigious awards is a strong motivating force behind their quality initiative.

The Deming Prize. Following Deming's lectures in Japan, the Japanese Union of Scientists and Engineers (JUSE) began awarding the Deming Prize in 1951 to companies with outstanding total quality programs. Today, a company that applies for the award must undergo a rigorous audit of its operations; this audit evaluates how well the management and control processes support quality products and services. In 1989 Florida Power & Electric became the first non-Japanese company to win the prize. Applying for the award is no easy task. "To win, [a company] must put a huge bureaucracy in place, write an application of up to 1,000 pages, and spend years working with the JUSE which administers the prize."[12]

Malcolm Baldrige National Quality Award. This award, managed by the U.S. Department of Commerce, was established in 1987 in honor of Malcolm C. Baldrige, the former Secretary of Commerce. The award is presented annually, recognizing companies that have successfully implemented total quality systems. A maximum of six companies can win an award, two each in manufacturing, service, and small business. One indication of the interest in total quality practices is that in 1990, over 180,000 applications were requested.[13]

Companies that apply are rigorously evaluated in the following seven categories (the 1992 weightings given to each category are shown):

Baldrige Examination Categories and Point Values

1. Leadership (90 points)
2. Information and analysis (80 points)
3. Strategic quality planning (60 points)
4. Human resource development and management (150 points)
5. Management of quality process (140 points)
6. Quality and operational results (180 points)
7. Customer focus and satisfaction (300 points)

Some of the past Baldrige Award winners include:

Manufacturing

GM, Cadillac Division
IBM, Rochester
Milliken & Company
Motorola
Westinghouse Commercial Nuclear Fuel Division
Xerox Business Products and Systems
Solectron Corporation
Zytec Corporation

Service

Federal Express Corporation

Small Business

Globe Metallurgical
Wallace Company
Marlow Industries

The Extent of the Quality Movement and Its Results

Spend some time in the halls of corporate America and you will quickly see that the quality movement is quite prevalent. The thousands of requests for the Baldrige Award applications alone attest to the interest companies are showing in quality. A recent General Accounting Office report shows that:[14]

- Out of 149 U.S. corporations that responded to a survey of senior executives at 800 of the largest corporations, 111 reported they had a quality management program in place.
- In that same survey, 62 companies indicated that they measured the impact of quality on profitability and 47 reported increased profits.
- Data from companies that had implemented quality management practices revealed:
  Increased job satisfaction
  Improved attendance
  Decreased employee turnover

       Improved quality products and services
       Greater customer satisfaction
       Improved market share and profitability

- Some common themes in these quality-focused organizations were:
  1. Corporate attention was focused on meeting customer requirements.
  2. Senior management led the way in building quality into the corporate culture.
  3. All employees were trained, empowered, and involved in efforts to continuously improve quality.
  4. Systematic processes throughout the entire organization were implemented to foster continuous improvement.

Lois's Story

Lois Hill is manager of guest services for the Harbortown Plaza Hotel, one of the thirty-five hotels owned by Chamberlain Hotels & Resorts Company (CH&R). She is responsible for three departments: reservations, front desk, and room services, and she reports directly to the hotel general manager. She has been in the hotel industry for ten years: three years with a CH&R competitor, four with a smaller CH&R property, and the last three years with the Harbortown Plaza. Her entire career has been in guest services, and she is quite proud of her accomplishments. Recently however, Lois has become threatened by tremendous changes at the hotel under what Nick Snowden, the general manager, calls "creating a total quality environment."

It all started when Nick returned from a three-week total quality workshop attended by all thirty-five CH&R general managers. To say that Nick came home committed to total quality was an understatement. Within a short time Nick was passing around a mission statement that would eventually have an effect on the entire staff.

HARBORTOWN PLAZA HOTEL
Mission Statement

The Harbortown Plaza Hotel is dedicated to surpassing our guests' expectations by providing exceptional, world-class quality service. Our challenge is to improve all aspects of internal and external customer satisfaction through the never-ending process of continuous improvement.

We recognize the importance of our guests and employees as our most valuable resource. We are committed to listening to and learning from their ideas. We strive to set the standards by which all other hotels, within and without CH&R, are judged.

Lois was finding it hard to go along with the quality program. Even though she had been told that training would be forthcoming, it hadn't started yet and she felt very confused. Her manager kept using terms she had never heard of, things like pareto charts, histograms, and cause and effect diagrams.

Lois felt vulnerable and defensive. She kept reflecting on the mission statement, the part about setting the standards against which all other hotels would be judged. That seemed to threaten her authority as a manager and the way she has been doing her job for the past ten years. It was made quite clear that from now on quality would be carefully measured, and she would be held accountable for various measures of guest satisfaction and employee satisfaction — measures that she was not sure were under her control.

Strategies for Employees

Whenever an organization puts a quality improvement program in place, many employees react with defensiveness; like Lois, they are working scared. But there are many things they can do to ease their sense of discomfort, and thus enjoy the rich pride that comes from doing quality work.

Understand the Need for Quality

In their book *Beyond Quality,* Jerry Bowles and Joshua Hammond note that until recently, U.S. companies generally agreed that 99 percent was an acceptable quality level; having 1 percent defective products, parts, or services was certainly reasonable—after all, it's only 1 percent.

But what does 1 percent really mean? Citing material from the American Society of Quality Control, Bowles and Hammond point out that if 99 percent performance is acceptable, then:[15]

- Doctors would write 200,000 inaccurate prescriptions each year.
- Drinking water would be unsafe four days out of every year.
- There would be no electricity, water, or heat for about fifteen minutes each day.
- For fifteen minutes every day, your telephone and television would not work.

Bowles and Hammond also tell a Texas Instruments (TI) story that goes back to the late 1970s. The company ordered a device from a Japanese supplier, announcing that the shipment of 1,000 must meet 99 percent acceptable quality level. "Several days ahead of the delivery date, two boxes—one large, one small—arrived along with a letter. The letter said in essence that TI would find 990 perfect devices in the large box and added, 'Although we're not sure why you want them, you'll find 10 defective devices in the small box.'"[16]

- *Getting better or getting beaten—the choice should be clear.* No organization—whether in manufacturing, service, or government—can afford the cost of poor quality. Certainly there are costs involved in implementing a quality system that strives to prevent defects. But the costs of the customer finding defects is much greater!

When Nick Snowden, the general manager of Harbortown Plaza, attended the quality training he clearly knew his hotel had to improve. They faced competition from the new hotels that had opened, and they faced an industry that was changing. The Harbortown Plaza was going to have to get better or it was going to get beaten. As he sat through the training, he also realized that Lois Hill was going to have to be a key player in the new direction.

• *Quality will get you competitive; being competitive is the best job security.* Are you concerned about whether your organization is as competitive as it used to be? How about your own job security — are you concerned about that? The two things are very closely linked, and the name of the link is quality. More and more organizations, faced with competition that did not exist in the past, are going to have to change. Business as usual may turn out to be no business at all! It's time to understand the importance of quality: quality service, quality products, quality processes.

• *Don't wait for training to answer all your questions; start learning on your own.* Start reading and learning about quality. There are plenty of materials available; check your manager's bookshelf, company training materials, or your local bookstore. The more you know, the less scary it becomes.

Think of it this way: no matter how well you think you are performing your present job, what could possibly happen if your performance improved? There is no penalty for becoming better.

Become Customer-Driven

• *If you are not meeting your customer's needs, it won't be long until someone else does.* Ultimately it is the customer that will determine quality. No matter what type of organization you work for or what type of job you hold, you must always remember that quality is defined by your *customer*. The customer should become the focus of everything you do. Find out what your customers need, how *they* define quality, and then *exceed* their expectations.

- *If you don't have a customer, you probably don't have a job.* You may have to broaden your thinking about what "a customer" is, but you certainly have one — everyone does. Whether you are a CEO, an investment banker, an accountant, a sales representative, an engineer, a computer programmer, a maintenance technician, or a machine operator, you have a customer. The question is, what types of customers do you have — external or internal?

External customers are the people who purchase your company's products or services. They are the reason your company exists. They pay the company bills, including your salary, and their needs should be the number-one priority. *Internal customers* are others in your company who depend on the work that you do in your department to do their own job. If you see your job as serving internal customers (other employees, other departments), you will ultimately increase external customer satisfaction as well.

- *Start viewing yourself from the perspective of your customers.* Try to stand in your customers' shoes. Ask yourself:
  Who are my customers?
  What do they need?
  What are their expectations of me?
  Am I giving them what they expect?
  How do I know how I am doing?
There are many ways to gather information from your customers, such as surveys, focus groups, or meetings.

Lois began to realize that her position as manager of guest services made her accountable for more customers than she cared to think about. She was responsible for every hotel guest who called for reservations, talked to the front desk, or used room service.

That wasn't all. She now realized that she also had *internal* customers: her employees. If she could better serve and communicate with her employees, she could positively affect the guests. Lois and Nick began working together to develop two

customer surveys: a guest satisfaction index to measure satisfaction with reservations, front desk, and room service, and an
abbreviated version of an employee attitude survey developed
at the corporate offices of CH&R.

She was now going to be held accountable for certain
aspects of guest satisfaction as well as employee satisfaction. It
was all pretty scary, but Lois had to admit that if she could effectively measure the data, and improve upon it, she could help
make Harbortown Plaza more competitive.

Make the Kaizen Commitment

> The real secret of Japanese success, perfected in vir-
> tual isolation over a forty-year period from the
> 1950s to the 1980s, is a customer-driven philosophy
> called "kaizen," or continuous improvement, im-
> plemented through a formal process of company-
> wide quality control.[17]

Too often organizations miss the fundamental concept of "continuous improvement" by worrying about tools and tactics. Don't
miss the forest by focusing on the trees. The strategies, tactics,
and tools associated with quality are valuable, but only if they
serve the underlying philosophy: that everything "deserves to
be constantly, patiently, incrementally improved."[18] Quality is
a process, and you must continually look to improve things as
a part of doing your job on a daily basis.

Lois realized she could begin developing her knowledge
base before the formal training started, and so she began doing
some reading about quality. As she learned more, she became
less anxious. She started seeing her job quite differently: she
began looking for ways to make improvements in the way she
was doing things—constant, incremental improvements.

Use the Tools to Gather Data

An important attribute of the quality process is the "willingness
to measure quality constantly and to identify and correct conditions causing poor quality."[19] You need to be sure that decisions
are based on facts, not opinion. And collecting and analyzing

facts involves one of the scariest aspects of quality: the tools. If you have never heard of them or used them before, they can be frightening indeed.

Lois was not an engineer, a statistician, or a quality control expert. "I never even liked math," she thought to herself. No wonder these tools she kept hearing about seemed so intimidating. However, through her company-sponsored quality training, she started to view some of these strange ideas as tools — instruments and strategies to help her improve quality.

The following user-friendly guide to "quality-speak" defines some of the many terms, tools, and techniques often associated with total quality programs. Once you are familiar with the lexicon, the tools and techniques are not so intimidating.

Acceptable Quality Level (AQL). AQL is the minimum number of acceptable items, usually stated as a percentage. Remember the earlier examples about 1 percent defects in such things as prescriptions and drinking water? That was an AQL of 99 percent.

Benchmarking. Continually measuring a company's products, services, and practices against those of its toughest competitors or the companies considered the world's best.

Cause and Effect Diagram. When a specific problem is identified, a cause and effect diagram helps separate the effects from the causes. Various categories of causes are examined, such as people, policies, materials, and machinery; then the most important causes are identified and selected for further analysis. When all the various causes are clearly specified, the diagram takes on the shape of fishbones and therefore is sometimes called a fishbone diagram. An example of a cause and effect diagram is shown in Figure 3.1.

Flow Charts. A flow chart is a visual representation of all the steps in a process. It depicts the flow of a product or piece of information from the beginning of the process to the end, and shows how the various steps are interrelated.

Just-in-Time (JIT). The process of having products, parts, or materials delivered at the exact moment they are needed — not earlier, not later. With just-in-time techniques, inventories can be reduced substantially.

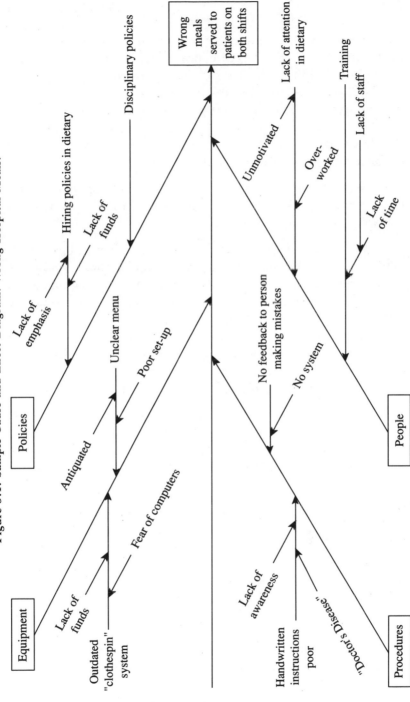

Figure 3.1. Sample Cause and Effect Diagram: Wrong Hospital Meals.

Reproduced with permission from *The Memory Jogger: a Pocket Guide of Tools for Continuous Improvement*, p. 24. Copyright © 1985 GOAL/QPC, 13 Branch Street, Methuen, MA 01844–1953. Tel: 508-685-3900.

Pareto Charts. Around the turn of the century, an Italian econo-
mist named Vilfredo Pareto claimed that in Italy 20 percent
of the population controlled 80 percent of the wealth. Today
the 80/20 ratio is useful to explain many business trends, including quality. Typically, 80 percent of a company's quality
problems stem from 20 percent of the causes. Pareto charts are
simple bar graphs that help rank order the various causes of
problems so priorities can be assigned.

Run Charts. These are simple line graphs that display observa-
tions over a period of time, such as sales per month, complaints
per week, or productivity per hour.

Six-Sigma Quality. A quality goal of 3.4 defects per million products — not only manufactured products but customer service as
well. A sigma stands for a standard deviation. One-sigma means
68 percent of products or services are acceptable; three-sigma
means 97.7 percent acceptable; six-sigma is 99.999997 percent
or 3.4 per million. Motorola, which has been striving to reach
six-sigma, estimates that through the effort it saved $500 mil-
lion in 1990. The six-sigma effort has also been joined by Digital, IBM, Corning, and Boeing, among others.[20]

Statistical Process Control (SPC). A method of analyzing measured
deviations in the production process in order to identify defects
before they occur. By analyzing where in the process these deviations occur, an organization is able to detect and eliminate
defects, thus reducing costs and at the same time increasing
productivity.

Learn to Separate Truth from Myth

One of the smartest things you can do to help yourself when
your company starts a quality program is work on changing
your mindset. You will hear many of your co-workers saying
things about quality that are simply not true, even though they
sound good. Learn to see these myths for what they are — the
defensive posture of people who are feeling threatened. Learn
to recognize the Seven Deadly Myths.

The Seven Deadly Myths of Quality

1.   Quality is just another fad; this too will pass. Think about it: How could quality be a fad? When was the last time you bought a product and you were totally unconcerned about quality? Quality is here to stay. Lois realized early on in the quality process that meeting the needs of her staff and in turn the hotel guests was simply good business.

2.   I don't have time to do this "quality stuff" and my regular work too. Do we have to do this? You bet! Today's consumers are much less willing to tolerate a bad meal, a defective product, or poor service. They expect quality, and they will go to the company that can give them the best product or service.

3.   Charts and graphs are for engineers. Lois used to think that charts and graphs were not relevant to her position as manager of guest services. But one day last week she changed her mind. Lois had been tracking guest satisfaction with a guest satisfaction index, which all guests were asked to complete before checking out. The push for quality was clearly having a positive effect on guest satisfaction, for the index was steadily climbing. Last week the site-selection committee for a major convention announced it had chosen the Harbortown Plaza, largely because of the impressive increase in guest satisfaction data. Lois was quickly becoming a believer in the tools of quality.

4.   I am a professional, I don't have customers. You may not have direct contact with the ultimate (external) customer, but you have internal customers. And remember, if you don't have customers, you probably don't have a job.

5.   What is wrong with the way we have been doing things? I am working in a quality way now. The issue is not that there is something wrong with the way you have been doing your job. The question you should be asking yourself is, "How can I do my job even better?" Remember: "There is no penalty for making a good thing better."[21]

6. *We aleady know what the customer wants; besides, we don't hear too many complaints.* How do you know what customers want? How are you measuring? You must make sure customer needs are identified on the basis of facts and data, not opinions. Also, by the time you hear customer complaints, it's too late. You may not hear a complaint — you simply lose the customer. The idea is to identify potential problems and prevent them from occurring in the first place. Lois knew she could not wait until she heard customer complaints; many guests would simply choose another hotel next time. Measuring customer satisfaction on a continuous basis was critical.

7. *Quality is a necessary evil.* Quality isn't evil but it *is* necessary. Quality is beyond necessary — your job may depend on it.

EMPLOYEE SUCCESS POINTERS
Achieving Success in a Quality-Focused Organization

➤ Don't wait for training to answer all your quality questions; start learning on your own.

➤ Identify your internal and external customers.

➤ Get a better understanding of your customers' requirements and expectations through surveys and meetings.

➤ Look for ways to make small, constant, incremental improvements in the way you do your job.

➤ Use the tools of quality to measure, identify, and correct poor quality.

➤ Understand that quality is here to stay.

Lois now fully supports the quality program. She clearly understands the importance of constant, continual improvement, particularly with regards to customer satisfaction. She knows the competition will be more than willing to provide exceptional customer service if the Harbortown Plaza doesn't. Now, as a manager, she needs to focus her attention on helping her staff achieve success in a quality environment.

Strategies for Managers

All those who study total quality, and those who have experienced it, agree on this: any new quality improvement program must have the complete support from the organization's management. Any manager who gives lip service to a mission of quality, but actually behaves in accordance with some of the seven myths, will sabotage the efforts of even the most quality-dedicated employees.

How, then, does a manager go about the job of managing in a way that supports and fosters a quality environment? Here we look at several specific things you can do. These efforts not only lead to higher quality, they also tend to reduce people's anxiety level. As Crosby has remarked: "Your employees will see more hope than fear in a well-planned, well-managed, quality improvement process."[22]

Empower Your Employees

Empowerment is the extent to which you give your employees the authority and responsibility to take actions on their jobs. Your employees can have the greatest effect on the quality process because they are the ones who perform the jobs on a daily basis. They are the experts. You must make sure your employees are involved in decisions that affect their jobs.

Lois, as manager of guest services, supervises employees who have a direct impact on the external customer, the hotel guests. When she worked with the general manager to develop the guest satisfaction index (GSX), she made sure her staff members were involved in the process, suggesting items to be included and dropping items they considered inappropriate. Once each month the employees are provided the GSX data for that month and previous months. The employees meet on their own to analyze the data. They continually try to come up with better customer service ideas that will improve the GSX data each month.

Lois has been amazed by the commitment her staff has put into improving quality at the Harbortown Plaza. For example, the room service staff members decided on their own that all room service orders will be delivered on time, as specified by the guest, or within twenty minutes of ordering. The front desk employees, at one of their meetings to review GSX data, made the commitment to have the fastest and friendliest check-in and check-out in the CH&R chain. The employees seemed to "own" their jobs and they were taking responsibility for them. And that's what empowerment is all about.

Encourage Open Communications

To ensure a climate where information is shared honestly and freely, it is critical that you have a system in place that allows for open communications. You must continually communicate with your work group to ensure that employees have the information, resources, and authority to accomplish their work.

Lois began conducting an employee attitude survey of her entire staff on a regular basis. After the employees filled out the survey, the data were summarized and returned to her. She was then expected to meet with them in small groups to look for ways to improve communications, and ask for more explicit feedback about how she was doing her job as their manager. The first time Lois had to conduct a feedback meeting, she was decidedly nervous. Still, she had to admit that there was probably a link between staff satisfaction and guest satisfaction.

It wasn't long before Lois became comfortable with the feedback process. She had real information about how her staff perceived her management style, and she realized that the process was a tool to help her improve as a manager. The feedback process also had a positive impact on employee turnover, which has always been a problem within several areas of guest services. Clearly, a more stable guest services staff would benefit the hotel guests.

Use Benchmarking

This technique involves studying what the best companies do in a particular practice or function and implementing their practices in your own organization. It is not a simple process of calling a few organizations and finding out what they do in a particular area. Rather, benchmarking is a systematic, continuous process of studying the products, services, and practices of your toughest competitors or those organizations that are known as being the best. Benchmarking is often done by teams, with up to twelve members. The team can take up to a year to make field trips and investigate several organizations, compare to their own, and make recommendations.

The idea is not just to compare to organizations in your own industry, but to the world leaders in a particular dimension. For example, Xerox, one of the leaders in benchmarking, compares itself to some of America's best:[23]

> American Express: billing and collection
> American Hospital Supply: automated inventory control
> Ford: manufacturing floor layout
> L.L. Bean, Hershey Foods, and Mary Kay Cosmetics: warehousing and distribution
> Westinghouse: Baldrige Award application process, warehouse controls, and bar coding
> Cummings Engine Company: daily production schedules

Xerox has developed a ten-step model for benchmarking that is used throughout the organization:[24]

1. Identify what is to be benchmarked.
2. Identify comparative companies.
3. Determine data collection method and collect data.
4. Determine current performance levels.
5. Determine future performance levels.
6. Communicate benchmark findings and gain acceptance.
7. Establish functional goals.
8. Develop action plans.
9. Implement specific actions and monitor progress.
10. Recalibrate benchmarks.

Champion the Quality Effort

Be enthusiastic about quality. Spend time talking about quality with your employees as well as your company's management.

Keep the quality effort alive by continually discussing, sharing, and learning about it. Show your commitment and enthusiasm by celebrating quality successes.

Lois remembered how apprehensive she was when the quality effort began at Harbortown Plaza, so she knew the importance of being positive. When she talked to her employees about quality issues, Lois let her excitement show. She communicated all successes that revolved around quality issues. Her enthusiasm was infectious. Her staff began to get excited and came to her with small successes surrounding quality. Her work group was always looking for ways to celebrate these successes. Quality was becoming a natural part of everyone's job.

Make Quality Happen

Quality improvement doesn't just happen; you, all other managers, and all employees *make* it happen. Your job as the manager is to structure the quality effort and to make sure that your employees have a clear understanding of the relationship between quality and their individual job responsibilities. One way to do that is through this five-step process for making quality happen in your work group.

1.   *Establish quality responsibilities and expectations with each employee.* Lois has begun meeting with all her employees on an individual basis to discuss the quality responsibilities and expectations that relate to their specific jobs. In these meetings, she stresses that quality is everyone's responsibility and everyone is accountable for it.

2.   *Agree on each employee's internal and external customers.* Lois and her employees, again on an individual basis, talk about the other employees and departments within the hotel (internal customers) that rely on their work, and what they expect. They also discuss how hotel guests (external customers) are affected by their individual job performance and what the guests expect. In many cases, this involves meeting with internal and external customers to discuss their expectations.

MANAGERIAL SUCCESS POINTERS
Achieving Success in a Quality-Focused Organization

➤ Empower your employees by giving them the authority and responsibility to take actions on their jobs.

➤ Put systems in place, such as employee surveys, that ensure information is shared honestly and freely.

➤ Find out what the best companies do in your particular area and implement these practices in your department.

➤ Champion the quality effort.

➤ Establish quality responsibilities and expectations for each of your employees.

➤ Establish a quality development plan with each employee, based on customer feedback.

---

3. Get feedback from customers on each employee's job performance. Lois regularly meets with customers to learn how employees are doing with the quality issues that were agreed to in step 1, and how they could all continue to improve. In the case of the guests (external customers), Lois contacts them by phone or sometimes in person when the customer is a frequent hotel guest. Each time Lois meets with an employee's customers, she shares that feedback with the employee.

4. Have employees assess their own progress. Lois meets with each employee at the end of the year. At this meeting, she asks the employees to assess their progress toward meeting their quality responsibilities and expectations. Any roadblocks that may have prevented them from meeting or exceeding expectations are also discussed.

5. Establish a quality development plan with each employee. At the end of the year, Lois meets with each employee. Together they generate and agree upon a quality development plan for that employee. The plan is based on inputs from the employee (step 4), Lois, and the internal and external customers (step 3). The plan outlines actions that will be taken over the coming year, focusing on opportunities for both the employee and the hotel to improve quality.

Achieving quality is the responsibility of everyone in the organization, not just one group or another. Most of us know that, and yet there is a tendency sometimes to blame poor quality on the other guy. Not long ago, the *Wall Street Journal* reported two surveys just three weeks apart. In one survey, workers at twelve major companies overwhelmingly insisted they were personally committed to meeting quality standards, but said the managers are to blame when quality is poor because *they* are not driven by quality. The second survey reported that many of the nation's top executives blame the lagging quality of American goods and services not on themselves but on a lack of commitment from workers.[25]

There is enough blame to go around. It is time to stop blaming and do something about it. We've all talked the talk, now let's walk the walk. Whether you are a manager or an employee, you can be the first step in building a quality work environment.

FOUR

Surviving During
a Downsizing

"Business is awful. Will I be laid off?" If you are thinking this way, you have lots of company. Downsizing, layoffs, reduction in force — whatever we call it, it has affected a staggering number of jobs.

In the early 1980s, downsizing had its main impact on blue-collar employees working for manufacturing organizations. In recent years, the scope of downsizing has broadened considerably and now includes white-collar employees working as middle-level managers, professional staff, office people, and high-level executives. These white-collar employees work not only for manufacturing firms but service, government, and high-tech organizations as well.

In fact, recent statistics indicate that organizational downsizing has shifted emphasis from blue- to white-collar positions. Let's take a closer look at the reality of downsizing:

- Between August 1989 and May 1990, 65 percent of the half million newly unemployed U.S. workers were managers, staffers, and professionals.[1]
- Over one million managerial and professional staff positions have been lost from 1979 to mid-1990.[2]
- In the first quarter of 1990, major American companies cut 110,000 staff positions.[3]
- Of the nearly 81,000 positions eliminated in 1,219 U.S. corporations between July 1989 and June 1990, about 45 percent of them were managerial or professional positions, up from roughly 34 percent a year before.[4]

73

- United Airlines has cut 25 percent of its staff.[5]
- DuPont has cut 50 percent of its executive positions at the level of vice president and above.[6]
- General Electric has eliminated five out of nine layers of management.[7]

   If we examine recent statistics for white- and blue-collar jobs together, the figures are enormous.

- Downsizing in the United States has increased from an estimated 2 million manufacturing jobs lost in the early 1980s to 3.2 million jobs at the end of that decade.[8]
- A survey conducted by the American Management Association revealed that 66 percent of organizations with more than 5,000 employees reduced their work forces in the second half of the 1980s.[9]
- Among the numerous cases of large-scale downsizing during the 1980s, Citibank cut 17,000 jobs, AT&T cut more than 32,000, and General Electric 105,000.[10]

   Forecasts of the 1990s suggest that downsizing will continue in all types and sizes of organizations. General Motors plans to eliminate 74,000 jobs, and the commercial banking industry may lose as many as 300,000.[11] In contrast to its long-honored practice of no layoffs, IBM started cutting jobs during the early 1990s.[12] Even the armed forces are not immune, with plans to cut over 30 percent of its military personnel by 1995.[13]
   Why are so many firms downsizing? Although the answer for a particular organization can be quite complicated, downsizing is normally caused by one or more of the following factors:

   Eroding market share
   International competition
   Domestic competition
   Increasing labor costs
   Obsolete plants, technologies, or products
   Poor management
   Poor labor-management relations

Regardless of the causes, it is important for all of us to realize that "job security" is a cruel oxymoron. It's debatable whether job security ever was real, but it certainly isn't as real as it was a generation ago. For most of us, our paycheck is as secure as our company's next quarterly report. Certainly, there are still jobs protected by union contracts and civil service, but they are becoming an endangered species.

Of all the reasons why people may be working scared, the fear that they'll be the next to go is one of the worst.

Terry's Story

Terry Wilson is a customer service representative (CSR) employed by a large American automobile company. Terry's job involves listening to and solving all types of complaints from car owners; all complaints come by phone. Terry and the other CSRs report to Nelson Richards, manager of customer service.

Terry is twenty-eight years old and has been employed by the company for seven years; this is her only job since college. Although dealing with irate customers is quite stressful, Terry finds the position challenging and rewarding. She'd like to stay with this auto company and eventually move up the corporate ladder.

Terry's profile is typical of most of the CSRs. They're in their late twenties or early thirties, it's their first job out of college, and they want very much to succeed.

They're alike in another way too: they're all working scared. The company has tried to control costs through non-layoff alternatives such as hiring freezes and early-retirement programs, but this strategy hasn't been enough to control costs and quite a few people have been laid off in the last few years.

Last year, five of the forty CSRs were laid off. Terry is close friends with two of them and feels depressed and frustrated. Both were good CSRs; why were they chosen for layoff? Why not others? Why not herself?

Nelson Richards has told the CSRs that their jobs are critical to the company's total quality management program and that their jobs are "about as secure as anyone's." Nevertheless,

Terry is very nervous; she hasn't built up a sense of her worth within the organization and lacks self-confidence because she still believes that she has much to learn. She believes that it's only a matter of time before she'll be let go.

Terry is not unique in her anxiety. Richards has noted that he hears a lot more rumors than ever before, rumors that too often become exaggerated and distorted. He has also commented that the CSRs seem to be looking out for themselves more than ever and, at the same time, banding together in small cliques. This has caused less cooperation among the CSRs and more backbiting. Productivity, measured by number of complaints handled successfully, has also decreased since the CSRs have been wasting time in gossip sessions.

Strategies for Employees

Are there strategies Terry can use to help her cope with her fears and save her job? Absolutely — it's what this section is all about. Working successfully in a climate of fear presents some emotional issues and some practical ones. Here we will look at many things that Terry can do to deal with both kinds of issues.

Acknowledge Your Feelings

Whenever any organization downsizes, it violates two fundamental motivating precepts: the need for security and the desire for justice. Clearly, downsizing poses a threat to the survivors' sense of security; now they're afraid that they may be among the next to go. It also violates their desire for fairness; survivors usually identify with the laid-off employees rather than with the company. The survivors find it difficult to understand how their company could be so callous and disloyal to these individuals.

It's important that you, as a survivor, not ignore or deny your natural feelings. Only through acknowledging and understanding them can you hope to reestablish your own sense of security and fairness. Take advantage of the support of others (such as co-workers, friends, family, and managers). At the same time, learn to recognize these four feelings brought on by downsizing, and give yourself time to get over them:

1. *Sadness.* It's depressing for survivors to see their friends and associates being asked to leave the company. Terry is upset because two of her close friends were laid off last year and she's not really certain why.
2. *Role ambiguity.* Ever since others have left, the survivors' jobs have changed and they're unsure about their new responsibilities and what management now expects of them. Terry's workload has increased since last year's downsizing, and she is not sure whether Mr. Richards feels that she is handling the changes well.
3. *Distrust.* People have seen competent employees let go in the past and now wonder whether management can be trusted to keep its word. Mr. Richards has told Terry that her job is as secure as anyone's, but Terry isn't sure she believes that.
4. *Caution.* Survivors become very cautious. They're so afraid to make mistakes that risk taking and innovation shrink down to zero. Terry feels that it's best for her to play it safe and not take any risks or do anything that might jeopardize her job.

Terry needs to talk over these feelings with others with whom she feels comfortable. She will learn that others feel the same way and that what she feels is normal.

Keep Rumors in Perspective

Rumors occur simply because we're human and we need to do something, anything, to relieve our fears. You can expect to hear rumors anywhere — in the hallway, restroom, break room, cafeteria, or parking lot. The rumors themselves hardly ever involve employee's names. Instead, rumors are about functional areas. "I heard that customer service is going to get trimmed, but sales and engineering are going to be saved."

Don't ignore rumors — they are an important source of information. No matter how bizarre or painful, rumors will help you to better understand your company's cultural temperature. But don't get obsessed by them either. Keep listening, but keep your perspective. Don't spend so much time worrying about rumors that you overlook doing your job.

The most important thing about rumors is this: remain rational. Listen to everything, but don't believe everything you hear. Always consider the source. When you hear a rumor from someone, stop and ask yourself two key questions: Can I trust this person to tell me the truth? Does this individual have anything to gain from telling me this? If the answers make you uneasy, then you need to verify the information with trustworthy sources such as co-workers who are your friends.

Does it make sense to check rumors with your boss? Although the answer depends somewhat on your personal relationship with your boss, you should know that this is usually a very tricky area. If your manager is involved in making difficult downsizing decisions, she or he can't say anything to you. From a legal standpoint, managers have to be extremely careful about what they say, especially when termination is involved.

But that doesn't mean you have to keep totally silent. You can certainly discuss the rumors with family and friends — and you should. If downsizing eventually affects you, and you haven't at least prepared them for the possibility, they can be devastated. Besides, your family and friends are your best source of support. Discussing rumors and fears with those we're close to is an excellent way of reducing stress.

Terry will continue to listen to the rumors but also take into consideration their source before taking them seriously. She realizes that her primary concern must always be her level of job performance and that she cannot let "doing rumors" interfere with doing her work.

Maintain a Positive Attitude

While downsizing has more direct implications for those employees who actually lose their jobs, the survivors will also be enormously affected. As a survivor, you are relieved that your position was spared and that you are still employed. However, once your initial relief is over, you find yourself having to cope with one or more of these consequences:

- *You are now expected to handle more responsibility.* You may be given job responsibilities formerly held by two, three, or even four other people. You feel overburdened and unsure what's expected of you. Terry's customer load has doubled during the past year. She can't afford to spend more than ten minutes on the phone with any single customer, and she worries that she may seem abrupt and rude to customers.
- *You might be transferred.* You may be relocated to another town, city, or state. This can be threatening to you, devastating to your spouse and children.
- *You could be demoted.* To remain with the organization, you may have to accept a job one or two levels below your present position, with a salary reduction and the need for retraining.

In addition to these tangible changes, many survivors struggle with confusion and feelings of betrayal. They might observe that more lower-level than upper-level employees have been terminated, that employees received no advanced notice of their layoffs, that management didn't keep them informed about the downsizing process, that the rules used to choose those to be laid off weren't fair, and that the company doesn't provide adequate caretaking activities to help individuals cope with the layoff.

Although their circumstances are different, survivors share the same feelings, many of them negative.

- Decreased trust. "I don't believe what management says."
- Decreased commitment to the organization. "I don't care what happens to this company."
- Decreased job satisfaction. "I don't like the work I do."
- Decreased productivity. "I do just enough to get by."
- Decreased self-esteem. "I don't feel as good about myself since I've been demoted; I'd really be devastated now if I also lost my job."
- Increased insecurity. "I'm probably on the list to go next."
- Increased role conflict. "I'm getting conflicting orders and I don't know who to listen to."
- Increased ambiguity. "I'm confused about what's now expected of me on my job."

• Increased sense of overload. "I'm so overworked; I'm always trying to catch up."

Of course these negative feelings are understandable. But you have to fight against them. They aren't doing you any good, and if they affect your job performance, they could do great harm. Let's look at several ways that survivors like Terry can convert their negative attitudes into positive ones.

Try to Be Upbeat. Several research studies have shown that job satisfaction can be more a result of how one's co-workers react to the job than the actual characteristics of the job itself.[14] By the way you talk about the job, you and your co-workers reinforce one another, either positively or negatively.

You can help improve the atmosphere by emphasizing to your peers the positive feature of your job, and deemphasizing the negatives. This will eventually help to increase their level of job satisfaction, which in turn will rebound on you. Terry makes it a point to talk about the great pay and benefits she and the other CSRs receive.

Focus on Job Enrichment. Unfortunately, downsizing too often results in job enlargement: you are required to take on the work of people who were laid off. Often you are simply expected to do more of what you're already doing, more of the same; almost inevitably this leads to your feeling overloaded, which in turn leads to lower productivity.

As a survivor, what you must do is convert job enlargement to job enrichment. Turn your frustration into creative energy, and look for ways to make the job more interesting, challenging, and stimulating. Try to see your job from a different perspective. Now that you're doing more work, do you have the opportunity to learn new skills?

Another thing you can do is talk with your manager about more autonomy. If you are given the authority to handle problems on your own, without having to stop and check with others, chances are you can do the work faster. This often has the effect of reducing the overall workload, and it certainly increases your satisfaction with the job.

Protect Your Ego. You cannot let your belief in yourself get away from you. Here are some things that you should keep in mind when you're feeling low.

- You're darn good at your job, and there are a lot of less productive people who will be let go before you. The more accurate your company's performance appraisal system, the better the chances that the weaker performers will be identified and laid off first.
- Remember that being demoted or laid off no longer has the stigma it once did. Even if you should be laid off, a prospective future employer is not going to assume it was because of incompetence.

Stay Busy. Finally, maintaining a positive attitude means not letting your job performance fall off, no matter how scared you are or how discouraged you might be. Focus your attention on showing management that you're indispensable.

Terry has made up her mind that she's going to maintain a positive attitude. She's thankful that she has a job that she enjoys. Car sales have increased lately, and she's hopeful that this trend will continue and that no further layoffs will be needed. She knows that, although she's still learning, she is one of the better CSRs. If she's laid off, there's nothing to be embarrassed about. She'll just have to look for, and find, a comparable position. She hopes that looking at the glass of water as half full instead of half empty will help not only her, but her fellow CSRs as well.

Prove Your Worth

It almost goes without saying that you need to perform your normal, everyday job duties effectively. But more important, you've got to find ways to make yourself more valuable to your company.

Here's what Terry did. Rather than continuing to feel insecure about her value to the company, Terry decided to do something proactive to save her job and feel better about herself.

Terry used her innovativeness and creativity to start new intracompany communication processes. One of the main duties of the customer service reps is listening to customers. This allows them to gather a great deal of customer information. In the past, it has sometimes been very difficult to disseminate this information appropriately throughout the rest of the company. In her particular area, Terry got a lot of technical information from customers. She took it upon herself to design a way to meet with the engineering staff in the company to distribute this information to them. After a while, her communication process was being used by all the other CSRs. Terry's idea was perceived by Nelson Richards and other company managers as a real "value added."

Protect Yourself

You'll be doing yourself a big favor if you realize this: your company isn't going to take care of you. The days of coming to the front door of large companies and seeing an invisible sign reading A JOB FOR LIFE are gone. Accepting this reality is the first and most crucial step to survival in today's times. Once you accept the fact that there is no longer any guaranteed job security, you will do what needs to be done — protect yourself by putting your career in your own hands.

You need to seriously take stock of your current job situation. You can do this by thinking about the answers to the following key questions:

Does my job feel secure?
Are there opportunities for advancement?
Am I learning new things that can help me advance?
Do I like working with my manager?
Do I like working with my co-workers?
Do I enjoy doing the work itself?

If you're not satisfied and secure, it may be time to start a job search. And do it *now*, while you're still working.

Regardless of how you feel about your current position,

you owe it to yourself to come up with a plan for what you would do if you're let go. Anticipating how you would cope if you were let go not only builds your self-confidence but also gives you time to prepare yourself by doing such things as enrolling in classes, attending training programs, or even starting a second job.

Terry has taken stock of her current job situation. Although there are few opportunities for promotion and her job security is shaky, she likes her work, her co-workers, and her manager. Her "what would I do next?" plan is to look for a CSR position in the service industry. For instance, she has always liked the hotel and restaurant businesses. She's also decided to continue her education and is working toward her MBA degree at night. In the meantime, she has not been shy about letting others in the division know about her innovative intracompany communication process.

What else could Terry be doing to protect herself? Here are some ideas:

- *Stay visible.* Terry should continue to let others know what she is doing and what she's accomplishing. Don't forget: out of sight, out of mind.
- *Stick to your knitting.* Terry must keep her head down and stick to the work she does best. She should not waste much time getting embroiled in office politics and rumors.
- *Document your accomplishments.* Terry should keep track of her key activities on projects, conversations with superiors, and accomplishments. This information might come in handy when personnel decisions are made.

Strategies for Managers

People who survive a downsizing are in a very difficult position. They usually have more work to do, and they are expected to do it in an atmosphere of fear and distrust. Is it any wonder their productivity slips?

No one should be expected to cope with this situation without help from the manager. It is the manager's job to help

---

EMPLOYEE SUCCESS POINTERS
Achieving Success in an
Organization That Is Downsizing

➤ Acknowledge your feelings of sadness, role ambiguity, distrust, and cautiousness.

➤ It is wise to be aware of rumors, but don't let them overpower you.

➤ Try to be as upbeat as you can.

➤ Look for opportunities to enrich your job by making it more interesting, stimulating, and challenging.

➤ Work on maintaining a healthy level of self-esteem.

➤ Don't let your job performance fall off, no matter how scared or discouraged you might be.

➤ Look for special things to do to prove your worth to your company.

➤ Come up with a "what would I do next" plan.

➤ Take stock of your current job situation; if you're not satisfied or secure, begin a job search.

➤ Protect yourself by staying visible, sticking to your knitting, and documenting your accomplishments.

---

employees deal with the negative emotions and to find new commitment and motivation for doing quality work. Here we look at some of the things managers can do to help the survivors.

Provide as Much Information as Possible

At this critical time, the manager needs to be perceived as the calm at the center of the storm. More than anything else, this means communicating as much information as possible to your employees.

First, you must confidently explain to employees what has happened, why it's happened, and why the company is on the right track. Employees are more willing to accept immediate injustices if they can see how their company's actions will contribute to long-term benefits for themselves and others.

Second, you must find ways of heading off rumors. Employees will talk about what they *think* is going on in the organization. If they're not given real information, then they'll simply create and pass on rumors. Mr. Nelson, Terry's manager, installed a "rumor board" outside his office. If Terry hears a rumor, she can write it up and post it on the rumor board. Within twenty-four hours, Mr. Nelson posts the real facts pertaining to the issue next to the rumor. Rumors spread quickly, and it's therefore important that employees be told the truth, even if the truth is that studies are being conducted and no final decisions have been made as yet.

Third, you must clarify what you expect from each employee from now on. The survivors are worried about their increased workloads and unfamiliar job responsibilities. Mr. Richards met individually and privately with all the CSRs, to explain exactly what they will be expected to do, how they will do it, and with whom they'll interact.

You must also realize that to a large extent the survivors are entering a new organization. Simply informing them of their new responsibilities isn't enough. You need to explain in detail how they will be helped to adapt to their new tasks and responsibilities through training, mentoring, and coaching.

Show Some Compassion

Survivors of downsizing need TLC. Fortunately, there are several things you can do during this stressful period to demonstrate compassion. For one thing, let your employees know that you realize the hardships imposed on them by the downsizing, and that you regret it. It also helps to meet with employees, either in small groups or individually, to give them an opportunity to vent their feelings of frustration, shock, sorrow, and anger.

Certain employees need time and help to work through the guilt they're feeling because they managed to survive while their friends didn't. This is the time when you must build on the survivors' feelings of self-worth and security. Help them to understand that there were good reasons they were chosen to remain while others were dismissed. This means showing them how their expertise will contribute to departmental and company goals. It also means telling them that tangible rewards, such as merit increases, will continue to be tied to outstanding performance. It does *not* mean promising them that downsizing will never happen again.

It also does *not* mean attempting to motivate them through fear tactics. One chief operating officer of a company that had downsized remarked, "After the downsizing, I brought all my remaining VPs together and told them that there are still some of them who won't be ready to go where we will need to go to be profitable, unless they buckle down." What happened? Risk taking and innovation have virtually disappeared — managerial characteristics this company must have to remain competitive. Instead, playing it safe and passing the buck have become the company's prevailing style.

Compassion for employees who had to leave is critical, too. How they are treated will have a lasting effect on those who stay. It's the first and probably their most important impression of the downsizing. As the manager, do everything in your power to see that the layoffs are handled professionally and compassionately. At a minimum, this should involve adequate financial and benefits severance packages. Outplacement assistance is essential. This might mean nothing more than helping laid-off employees prepare a résumé and register with their state employment service. In full-scale programs, normally conducted by outplacement consulting firms hired by the downsizing company, experienced counselors help laid-off employees work through the shock of job loss and support them in their search for another job or career transition.

Consider Alternatives

There are lots of alternatives to downsizing:

- Reduce the work week.
- Offer an attractive early retirement program.
- Institute across-the-board salary cuts.
- Trim spending waste.
- Retrain existing employees.
- Use voluntary layoff programs.

If the decision is in your hands, seriously consider these alternatives before deciding to lay people off. If it's not in your hands, try to offer them as suggestions to senior management.

Two of the furniture industry's leading performers, Herman Miller and Steelcase, reported recently that they have found a better option than forced layoffs. Rather than indiscriminately pruning their staffs, both companies have turned to using voluntary leave programs to cut their expenses. Two hundred Herman Miller employees are on voluntary leaves of up to several weeks, and Steelcase has asked almost half of its 6,500 hourly employees to take up to two months leave of absence at reduced pay.[15]

It's important to remember that downsizing through layoffs often doesn't work. In a four-year study of downsizing in thirty manufacturing organizations between 1986 and 1990, it was found that only five or six showed a marked increased in productivity. In all the other cases, performance went down.[16] Why? In almost every case, downsizing reduced employee loyalty, confidence, morale, commitment, innovativeness, trust, and participation; and increased conflict, scapegoating, fear, secretiveness, politicking, and bureaucratization. These companies would have been much better off to consider other alternatives.

Nelson Richards has had several group meetings with Terry and the other CSRs to explain what has happened. At one of these meetings, he expressed his regret that they have to work harder and be under more stress. Terry and her co-workers appreciated his concern. He has also continued to use his rumor board to correct rumors before they get out of hand. He has met privately with Terry to recognize her accomplishments and to discuss and clarify performance expectations. Mr. Richards and other managers in the customer relations division

hope that no more cost cutting will be needed this coming year.
If it is, they intend to use a reduced work week rather than lay-
ing off additional people.

MANAGERIAL SUCCESS POINTERS
Achieving Success in an
Organization That Is Downsizing

➤ Explain to employees what has happened, why it has happened, and why you believe the organization is on the right
track.

➤ Find ways to head off rumors.

➤ Explain to each of the survivors what you expect from each
of them with respect to their increased workloads and new
responsibilities.

➤ Acknowledge the hardships imposed on your employees by
the downsizing.

➤ Give your employees an opportunity to vent their feelings
of frustration, shock, sorrow, and anger.

➤ Refrain from making promises that you might not be able to
keep, such as "downsizing won't happen."

➤ Build the survivors' feelings of self-worth and security by letting them know that there were good reasons for choosing
them to remain.

➤ Make outplacement assistance available to employees.

➤ Consider alternatives to downsizing before deciding to let
valuable employees go.

FIVE

Staying Flexible During Mergers and Acquisitions

You heard the rumors for the first time about three months ago, but you didn't really think it would happen. Last Friday it was announced — a large corporation has acquired the company that has been such an important part of your life for the past nine years. There seem to be lots of questions and few answers.

Will you be able to keep your job?
Will the organization's expectations of you change?
Will you be transferred to another location?
Will you be demoted?
Will you lose your accumulated benefits?
Who will you be reporting to in the new organization?
How will decisions get made?
Will that job assignment or promotion you were promised
  be honored?
Will your pay be affected?
How will redundancies in staff positions be handled?

Are you working scared? You bet. If it's any comfort, you are not alone. The list of companies involved in mergers and acquisitions (M&A) looks like the "Who's Who" of American business: Gulf and Chevron, General Electric and RCA, General Foods and Philip Morris, R. J. Reynolds and Nabisco, Wells Fargo Bank and Crocker Bank, Burroughs and Sperry, AT&T and NCR — the list goes on and on.

The 1980s can be described as the decade of "merger

mania"; some 35,000 publicly traded firms were sold for a total of $1.3 trillion. And the trend continues. In 1990 there were 3,972 M&A transactions at a total cost of $171.4 billion.[1] To put things in perspective from an employee standpoint, it is estimated that from 1980 to 1990, in the financial industry alone, 3,400 banks and savings and loan institutions were involved in mergers affecting the lives of 822,000 employees.[2]

For both strategic and global reasons, M&A's will be with us throughout the decade to the year 2000. Companies are using M&A's as a strategy to achieve organizational growth. They are growing and expanding simply by acquiring new companies. Also, buying foreign companies is a way of expanding into the international arena. Sometimes a U.S. corporation acquires a foreign organization; in other cases a foreign corporation buys a U.S. company.

A word about terminology: throughout the chapter we will be using the terms *M&A, merger,* and *acquisition* interchangeably. There is a tendency for the smaller company to view the transaction as a merger, whereas the larger organization typically views the arrangement as an acquisition. Our emphasis in this chapter will be on the company that has been acquired by a larger organization. Nevertheless, from an employee perspective the issues are similar. No matter which side of the fence they are on, employees are working scared.

Jeff's Story

Jeff Martin had been working for a manufacturer of consumer products for the past nine years. Jeff had always loved working for the company. It had always been truly interested in developing employees. It was a low-key, nonpolitical organization that employees often described as being "kinder and gentler" than the typical organization of its size. Most of the 12,000 employees worked in facilities that could best be described as "pastoral settings located in the middle of the woods," and this seemed to fit the culture of the organization.

Then came the announcement: they were being acquired by a much larger organization—a competitor, no less.

When Jeff looks back on it now, he can identify five stages that the M&A process went through.[3] In his own words, Jeff describes these five stages.

Stage 1: The Bomb Drops. "Everyone knew where they were when they heard about the merger for the first time. Some employees were in their cars and they heard it on the radio, others were in meetings. I was in my office. I remember looking around, feeling like all the blood was just drained from my face. 'Shock' and 'disbelief' are the words that come to mind. I started to think about how much larger the organization was that we were merging with. I knew that many of the things about my organization's culture that meant so much to me were going to change. I was scared!

"About that time I heard someone else describe an M&A this way:

'For the sake of analogy, imagine that it is France, 1940. Paris has just fallen. The occupying forces are coming and the radio daily reports their troop movements. The end of a way of life is near. We can only wait.

'And imagine seeing some of our colleagues trying to anticipate the whims of the occupying force and scheming to ingratiate themselves with them. It is Vichy France psychologically revisited.'[4]

Stage 2: Preoccupation. "All of us were obsessed with the merger. It was all we could think about; it was all we would talk about. It certainly did not help our productivity. I remember looking around at all my filing cabinets, bookshelves, and company reports and thinking that all my past work could now be meaningless. Tension and chaos were in the air as we waited for the conquerors to arrive."

Stage 3: The Culture Clash. "They arrived. Some key new organizational members were added to the organizational chart. And of course when they arrived they also had all the answers.

'Arrogance' was the word that comes to mind. They were going to show us how to really run a company. There were big differences between the way the two companies did business and it became quite clear that they wanted their way to become our way."

Stage 4: Let the Purging Begin. "We were told that as a result of the merger, there would be a reduction in force of 20 percent of our work force. They kept stressing that 80 percent of us would not be affected, but of course 100 percent of us were worried. Some of our best talent left the company on their own, and others seemed to be let go for reasons we never really understood."

Stage 5: Merging and Emerging. "We realized that we were the survivors, and it was time to get away from the we versus they, the attack and defend, and the win versus lose mentality if the merger was going to be successful. I also remember reading about a survey of executives who had been involved with M&A's during a recent one-year period; 85 percent of them believed that 'people problems' had a greater influence on the long-term success of mergers and acquisitions than financial problems.[5] I was determined not to be one of the people problems."

Strategies for Employees

How can you be successful amidst merger and acquisitions? Let's take a look at some solutions.

Expect Change

If you thought there were a lot of changes going on before the merger took place, just wait—you haven't seen anything yet! There will be changes in the organizational culture, your job, and your co-workers. Change can no longer be thought of as a short-term reaction to a crisis or new competition, but rather a fact of today's organizational life.

Changes in Organizational Culture. There are going to be different priorities within the new organization. What was important in the past may not be as important now. There may be a new emphasis on customer service or quality. Values and traditions will probably change. For example, employees often complain that after a merger there was an overemphasis on profits at the expense of people. It should not be surprising, considering that top management is trying to prove they were right to suggest the merger to begin with.

You will also see changes in the way decisions are made. Expect mixed messages with regard to how much you will be involved in decision making. On the one hand, there may be a lot of listening and shared decision making. On the other, there will be very autocratic decisions handed down by top management in response to the pressures of profitability.

Changes in Your Job. Your job title may not change, but your responsibilities and actual job duties probably will. Be prepared to have changes move in one of two directions. The first is that you will have less responsibility. Instead of supervising the work, you are now the one actually doing the work. It may be frustrating to realize that you have just taken what seems to be a step backward. Some employees report that they feel they are doing the jobs of people who were two levels below them in the old company. But a step backward in your job responsibilities may in fact be a step forward with regards to job security.

On the other hand, you could have *more* responsibility. The new organization is running "lean and mean." This is a real opportunity to show your talent to the new organization. Get your new role clarified, find out what is expected of you, and exceed their expectations! The reality may be that your opportunities are much greater after the acquisition than they were before.

Changes in Your Co-Workers. Friends and colleagues you truly enjoyed working with on a day-to-day basis may have been transferred or left the company. Get to know your new colleagues, share your job histories, and look for things that you have in common.

If you have a new boss from the other company, try to clarify as best as you can what is expected of you. Use your new boss to help provide your education in learning about the other company. Ask questions. Find out the do's and don'ts related to customers and other departments.

Three months ago Tom came over from the other company to manage the group that Jeff was part of for six years. Jeff's previous boss for the entire six years took early retirement. At first Jeff was apprehensive, but now he thinks having a new boss is one of the better things that has happened to him since the merger. Why? Because Tom has answers. He has given Jeff a tremendous education in the history and culture of the other company that he never would have been able to get in such a short time otherwise. Because Jeff was genuinely interested and willing to ask the right questions, he was able to function more successfully in the new organization.

So what's your bottom line? Expect change, be flexible, adapt. Organizational decision makers should see you as one who adapts well to change no matter where it occurs. Adjusting to change is critical to your success. Being inflexible, assuming there is no better way of doing things than the way they have been done in the past, is a sure way of failing. To *really* succeed in the new company, you need to do more than accommodate change. You should be seen as a change agent. Employees who respond to change by saying, "Things are going fine. If it ain't broke, don't fix it," are going to be stuck. To move ahead, you should be saying, "If it ain't broke, let's break it and make it better."

Learn How to Reduce Stress

Change causes stress — some changes more than others. Seeing your company swallowed up by another is stressful indeed and can affect you in many ways. M&A's create eight specific sources of stress:

1.   *Role overload.* You are told the organization must run "lean and mean" as a result of the merger. You understand how

that may help the short-term bottom line for the organization, but it is creating high levels of stress. You feel that you are assigned more work than you can possibly handle.

2. *Role ambiguity.* Because of all the changes going on in the organization, you no longer have a clear idea of what is expected of you. In the past, you were pretty clear on what the organization expected of you. Today, things seem about as clear as mud.

3. *Role conflict.* You are used to doing your job in a certain way and have been quite productive in the past. Now, however, employees in the company that acquired yours are acting like the "conquering heroes." They are telling you how to do things in a manner that you believe may not work well in your organization.

4. *Fear of job loss.* You realize it is quite common for merged and acquired companies to downsize. You have survived so far, but you are worried that you could be next.

5. *Politics and power struggles.* Everybody seems to be jockeying for position. Projects that were moving along now seem to have lost their funding. Politics rather than job performance seems to be the daily concern of co-workers, and it becomes very difficult to get your job done. Time and effort seem to be continually wasted on corporate politics.

6. *Infrequent feedback.* In the midst of all the turmoil, you are really putting in the effort and trying to do a good job. But you are given very little feedback about your job performance, resulting in greater stress.

7. *Autocratic leadership.* You seem to be left out of the decision-making loop on many issues that you were always part of in the past. The right *words* have always been there from the acquiring company, but the *actions* do not follow. You may be part of the "new family," but you are being treated like a stranger.

It seems that the leaders demand miracles but do not provide the necessary support.

  8. Career uncertainty. You no longer feel that the career opportunities that once existed are still realistic. There seem to be fewer opportunities for career growth than ever before.

  Exacerbating the eight stressors described above is the general organizational climate of ambiguity and uncertainty that takes over. This climate and the resulting information vacuum exist for several reasons:

1. Top management feels a need to be discreet until the merger is finalized.
2. Management does not have a clear sense of direction.
3. Management itself lacks information about the impact of the merger.
4. Everyone, including management, is suffering from fear of the unknown.

  Stress and uncertainty are facts of organizational life during M&A's. So what can you do? Learn how to manage what cannot be avoided. Here are some specific things you can do to manage the stress level.

  Learn Simple Meditation. Herbert Benson of the Harvard Medical School demystified the concept of meditation in his popular 1975 book, *The Relaxation Response.*[6]
  Jeff has really been stressed out since his company was acquired. After learning the Benson technique, he decided to try it. Here is his routine:

1. Jeff finds a quiet room and sits in a comfortable position. He doesn't lie down, for he might fall asleep.
2. He closes his eyes and takes a "what happens, happens" attitude.
3. He begins to deeply relax all muscles. He does this by tensing and then relaxing each muscle group, starting with his

fists, progressing up his arms to his head, and down his torso to his feet. He tries to keep his muscles completely relaxed.

4. He breathes through his nose, concentrating on his breathing. Then he says the word "one" silently to himself, on every outbreath. (It could be any word or phrase; it's simply a device to keep his mind from wandering.)

5. When distracting thoughts come into his mind, he simply allows them to "pass through" while he concentrates on repeating the word "one."

6. Jeff does not worry about how deeply he is relaxed while meditating. He knows that he cannot force the relaxing effects of meditation. He takes what he can get.

Jeff has found that he feels a sense of calm and relaxation after meditating. It only takes about ten minutes, but it seems to give him some control over his reaction to the various stressors he has been encountering at work.

Several studies have found that people who meditate recover from stress more rapidly than nonmeditators. Companies are starting to take note. Several have started or support meditation programs, in one form or another, including Coors Brewing, Monsanto Chemicals, Arthur D. Little, Xerox, Connecticut General Life Insurance Company, First National Bank of Chicago, and the U.S. Army.[7]

Strive for Balance in Your Life. Jeff's initial reaction to the M&A was to eat, think, breathe, and talk work. He thought the best thing he could do was to put off vacations and social events, and instead throw himself into work. He was wrong. That only made the stress worse.

Don't put your life on hold. Take planned vacations, go to special events that you look forward to, and exercise regularly. If you don't already have an exercise program, start one. In addition to the health and fitness benefits, physical exercise actually reduces stress.

Change Your Thinking. One of the most powerful methods of dealing with stress is analyzing and changing the way you think. The way you *think* about stress makes stress worse. We often make several mental errors that contribute to our stress level during M&A's.

- *Selective perception.* Once the M&A takes place, it is easy for you to assume that the organization is now a terrible place to work. You then start looking for all the reasons *why* it is a terrible place and ignore all evidence to the contrary.

- *Overgeneralizing.* "Since our company was acquired, I no longer have any supervisory responsibilities. Therefore, I must be worthless as a supervisor." This is an overgeneralization based on only one situation. The decision to take away supervisory responsibilities may have nothing to do with your abilities as a supervisor, but was simply companywide policy.

- *Catastrophizing.* You may have a tendency to blow the significance of negative events way out of proportion. "The way our company was before we were acquired was the best company I will ever work for. My job was the greatest job I will ever have. I'll never have another job that good. I'll never be as happy at work again."

How you think will determine how you behave. What are some ways of changing the way you think?

One way is to work on changing your self-talk. Examine carefully what you say when you mentally talk to yourself and notice those times when you are catastrophizing and blowing things out of proportion. You need to stop negative self-talk and start telling yourself positive things. Here are a few examples of positive self-talk.

> "I have had difficult situations at work before, and I have always done a good job of handling them. I know I can handle this one."
> "I'm going to concentrate on making the best out of the situation. I won't waste time worrying about things I have no control over."

"It seems bad now, but this could end up being the best thing that ever happened to me with regard to work. There may be new opportunities. Let's wait and see what happens."

Another thing you can do to change your thinking is to consider the worst-case scenario. Ask yourself, what is the worst possible thing that could happen to me? Are you going to die because your company was acquired by another? No. Are you going to lose your health? No. Are you going to go to jail? No. Are you going to lose your job? Maybe.

Now you have hit on the worst possible outcome. If you can accept this worst-case scenario, you are on the road to dealing with the situation successfully. You can now put things in perspective. You may even be saying to yourself that you were thinking about looking for another job anyway, and in the past whenever you changed jobs it was always a step up. You have now created a much healthier scenario.

Mentally Rehearse Your Actions. Imagining yourself in a stressful situation and rehearsing how you are going to handle it, before it happens, is another way to reduce stress. It involves practicing an upcoming stressful event in your head. Here again, the premise of the technique is that your attitudes and thoughts are going to affect your behaviors. The more positive and successful your thoughts, the more effective the actual behaviors.

Suppose you have to make a presentation to the acquiring company's top management team. It could have a tremendous impact on your career. Try to visualize the event in great detail, starting with what the room is like and what you're wearing. Run through the entire situation in your mind. Picture yourself being asked difficult questions and handling them successfully. Repeat this mental rehearsal several times until you begin to feel more comfortable with the upcoming presentation.

Become Part of the Solution, Not the Problem

No matter how large or small it is, the company you work for often becomes an important part of your personal identity. When that company is acquired by another larger organization, it loses its original identity and you therefore may feel part of *your* identity has been lost too. Like any big loss, the death of a company has five widely discussed stages. Learn to recognize them, and try to remember that this is a natural process and that it will end.

   1.   Denial. When Jeff first heard the rumor that the merger was about to take place, he refused to believe it. He continued to deny that the merger was actually happening. Somehow he believed his company would thwart off the merger. Even after the merger took place, he convinced himself that his company would be allowed to remain independent. Wishful thinking.

   2.   Anger. Then his reaction turned to anger. His energy now focused on the "evil empire" that was in the process of taking them over. How dare they destroy his world like that!

   3.   Bargaining. Jeff decided he must try to do something about it. He and some of his colleagues met with several key players from the other company. Their goal was to bargain with them to leave their part of the organization alone.

   4.   Depression. Jeff began to realize that all the bargaining in the world was not going to persuade the other organization to leave them alone; they wanted complete integration. Jeff and his co-workers were depressed. The old company was really gone, and they were going to miss it. They also realized that many others felt the same way, and they decided it was okay to mourn their loss. They decided to throw a rest-in-peace party. Everyone got T-shirts printed with "RIP" and the old company logo. They told stories, reminisced, laughed, and cried. When the party was over, most felt they had said goodbye to the old company.

   5.   Acceptance. It was time to face reality. Jeff began having a more positive attitude toward the other company. He became part of the solution, rather than part of the problem, by looking for ways the companies could more effectively integrate his department.

Try Not to Feel Guilty. Your friends and co-workers are going to leave for various reasons. Some will leave on their own and others will be asked to leave. Downsizing is not unusual; when Chevron acquired Gulf, almost 20,000 jobs were lost within one year.[8]

You may be one of the "stayers" and you may be thinking that some of the "leavers" were just as productive as you, if not more so. It's not your fault. Try not to feel guilty. Stay positive and focus on being as productive as possible. You must continually look to the future and not waste time perseverating on the past.

Also, don't feel guilty if you find yourself feeling sympathetic toward the "other guys." Your counterparts in the other company are not "the bad guys" but are in much the same boat you are. Employees in both companies probably heard of the merger at the same time, and both sides have less information about their future than they would like.

Set Goals. You may not know exactly how the merger will affect you yet, but now is the time to keep yourself motivated by setting goals for the near future. Here are a few points to keep in mind when setting goals:

• *Be specific.* Jeff knew that if he was going to keep himself motivated, he couldn't just decide he was going to "do his best." He set very specific key job goals, and gave each one a deadline. He kept these goals in a file on his desk so he would have easy access to them.

• *Stretch yourself.* Jeff made sure his goals were reasonably difficult to achieve—difficult but not impossible. He knew that, in this fashion, he would not only be more productive but also get a sense of accomplishment from achieving his goals.

• *Measure your results.* If the goal-setting process was going to keep Jeff motivated, he knew he had to make sure his

goals were measurable. Jeff set his goals based on what he wanted
to accomplish over the next three to six months. Then he set
short-term weekly goals so he could measure how he was doing
along the way.

Be a Positive Force. Throw your energies into being positive rather than focusing on what is upsetting and frustrating.
Don't continually look for what is wrong, but search for the positive. Often, employees report that M&A changes are more positive than they originally anticipated.

Know When to Hold and When to Fold

> "What a bunch of con artists! They told us that the
> performance record is the key to retention. Well,
> why did twenty-five of my co-workers get termi-
> nated because of redundancy? The other firm kept
> their own twenty-five people in what they refer to
> as redundant jobs."[9]

This person is understandably bitter but must not let that bitterness interfere with making good decisions. At what point do you
decide it is not worth it, that it's time to put your resume together?

Immediately after an M&A, there are typically going to
be short-term setbacks, but they should not be the basis for deciding to quit. The larger concern ought to be what you think is
going to happen one to two years down the road. Short-term
problems may be corrected and your career could be back on
track. It is important to understand that impulsive career moves
"made out of panic or other emotions are often poor moves."[10]

On the other hand, you may feel that the changes are unacceptable and you cannot be a positive force in helping the
merger along. It may be time to move on.

But remember, "never quit to quit — quit to start."[11] Will the
new job enhance at least one of the five following characteristics?

1. Provide you with more responsibility
2. Provide substantially higher pay

3. Provide more interesting daily activities
4. Involve less stress and anxiety
5. Be more psychologically rewarding

The bottom line is, don't psychologically remove yourself from your present position or announce your plans to leave until you have something else lined up. Make sure your productivity remains high. Even if you have already made a decision to find another job, you are going to need references from your current employer.

Get on Their Wavelength

Let's face it, whether you like it or not, the merger is a fact. To be successful, you should start learning as much as you can about the other side.

Jeff has decided to stay with the organization and has made a concerted effort to get to know the organization that acquired his company. The first thing he did was change his attitude. Before the acquisition, Jeff had always looked down on the other company; after all, they were a competitor. Now, however, he realized it was time to start looking for the positive in both the other company and its people. For the first time he realized they were all on the same team.

Next, Jeff started a crash course on learning as much about the other company as he could. He obtained past annual reports, company brochures, and newsletters. He even went to the human resource department and asked for employee orientation materials. He started talking to employees from the other company. He asked questions to learn as much as he could about the other company's history and its culture.

Finally, Jeff volunteered to serve on merger transition and integration teams. He realized that by being flexible and showing an eagerness to learn about the other side, he was not only increasing his chances for success but also turning the merger process into a genuine growth experience for himself. It also allowed him to get to know the other side, and allowed the other side to get to know him.

Recognize the Pitfalls

Achieving success amidst M&A's can be hampered by several pitfalls. Learn to recognize them, and you can take steps to avoid them. The seven pitfalls described here can be seen as a summary of the main themes of this chapter.

1. Ignoring the positive potential of the merger. Seeing everything about the merger in a negative light is going to hamper your success. Don't only look for the negative; search out the positive.

2. Making career decisions out of panic. As we have seen, during the initial phases of an M&A you may find yourself angry and depressed. Now is not the time to make long-term career decisions. Impulsive decisions often lead to poor consequences. Take the long view: what is best for you over the next couple of years?

3. Assigning all blame for your unpleasant feelings to the managers of the firm. Many of the current managers may have come from the company that acquired yours. You may be getting less information than you would like, and you may not have a clear idea of what is expected of you in this new environment. Do not take all your negative feelings out on the current managers. They may not know any more about the company's future plans than you. Seek out information, but do not expect the current managers to have all the answers.

4. Continually criticizing the merger and being seen as inflexible. One of the key behaviors that leads individuals to fail is being seen as inflexible. One manager had this to say: "We had a good idea from the start that Tom was probably not going to make it. He seemed to criticize every move we made. He was inflexible. Whatever his group did in the past was the *only* way of doing it. He just wasn't open to the possibility for change." As one vice president who has been through nine acquisitions put it, "Those individuals who achieve success during M&A's seem to be able to go with the flow."

5.   *Catastrophizing or blowing events out of proportion.* Things are tough enough; don't beat up on yourself. You may have less responsibility as a result of the M&A, but that certainly does not make you a failure or a poor employee. Truth is, it more than likely had nothing to do with *you.* Keep things in perspective.

6.   *Waiting for things to happen to you.* Don't sit around waiting for things to happen; do something. Ask questions, learn about the other company, and look for ways in which the other company accomplishes work activities similar to your own. Don't be on the outside of the M&A looking in; become a part of it.

7.   *Holding on to a "we vs. they" attitude.* You may feel betrayed as result of the M&A, you may not know what to expect, and your job security may be threatened. But *they* are not the enemy. If you are going to contribute to the success of the merger, and your career as well, don't think in terms of "we vs. they" but only *us.*

Strategies for Managers

Managers on both sides will find these success strategies can help their staff members adjust during the difficult transition period.

Overcommunicate. Make a conscious decision to communicate *more* than you think is necessary. Don't exceed the available facts, but make sure you communicate continually, with timely and comprehensive information. The more informed employees are, the more favorable their attitudes toward the merger will be.

Soon after the merger was announced, Jeff found that different managers worked through the process in very different ways. Sally Roberts, in particular, seemed to do an outstanding job of communicating with her work group. In group meetings, one on one, and in writing, she let them know what was happening. She gave them frequent updates, and she was always honest about organizational changes. In short, Sally was

---

EMPLOYEE SUCCESS POINTERS
Achieving Success Amidst Mergers and Acquisitions

➤ Expect change in your organizational culture, your job, and your co-workers.

➤ Manager your M&A stress through meditation, positive self-talk, and rehearsal.

➤ To keep yourself motivated, set work-related goals that are specific, reasonably difficult, and measurable.

➤ Look for the good in the situation; remain positive.

➤ Learn as much as you can about the other company.

➤ Don't make a career decision out of panic just to escape the M&A crisis.

➤ Keep things in perspective and don't blow negative events out of proportion.

---

able to counter any unfounded rumors by sharing information freely.

Become a Role Model. Publicize anything the two firms are doing together. Become a spokesperson for the merger and a role model for a positive attitude. Share everything you know about the acquiring firm's goals, values, and philosophies. Become a teacher in the characteristics of the acquiring firm. One employee said, "[Our manager] brought in material on the acquiring firm and even brought in three managers on his own to tell us about the firm. This really reduced my anxiety."[12]

Don't forget: as a manager, you have the greatest impact on what employees will think of the merger and how they will act. Your goal should be to help them "let go of the past by getting them excited about the future."[13]

Exhibit Leadership. Don't start playing it too safe. Remain a leader and a decision maker. Structure your employees' work and tell them what is expected of them. Make sure you let them know where they stand, and reward them for taking the initiative and not just playing it safe.

Make sure that the strategic preparation for the merger goes beyond the financial and business aspects of the transaction and focuses on the human implications as well. It is often the "people problems" that cause M&A's to fail.

Involve the Employees in the Change. The more you can get your employees involved in the changes, the more accepting they will be. Try and get your employees involved on integration teams. If your department is merging with a similar department in the other organization, ask employees to help. Allow them to share with you their ideas about the most effective ways of merging the two departments. Allow departmental employees to meet and put together what they consider to be their greatest strengths that will contribute to the success of the new department.

Become a Counselor. Give employees a chance to air their fears. Help provide support by making a conscious effort to be as visible as possible and answering all questions as soon as you can. Serve as a counselor and good listener to show you still value their opinions and ideas. Let the employees know that you realize that fear and anxiety are often an unfortunate by-product of M&A's. Wherever these feelings come from, let your employees know that you are willing to listen and discuss them.

Treat the Leavers with Dignity and the Stayers with Respect. How you treat the leavers will affect the stayers. It significantly colors their overall impression of the M&A. In addition, employees will feel guilty about being "survivors." Make sure that you acknowledge the experience that the stayers bring to the firm. Let them know that you respect and appreciate their years of service and that their experience and expertise will help make the new company more successful.

Don't Act Like a Conquering Hero. If you are a manager from the acquiring firm, you must be very careful about the impression you make with employees from the other company.

Jeff said that "some of the managers from the other company acted after the merger like they were the conquering heroes. They were going to show us how naive we were about the way we did our jobs. There was only one right way to do our jobs and it was their way. We were constantly told how flexible *we* needed to be, but *they* were totally inflexible."

Remember, acting like a conquering hero will have a negative effect on how you communicate, how you lead, and ultimately, how successful you are at managing during the M&A.

Jeff felt Sally Roberts did an outstanding job in this area. He reported, "Sally calmed many people down. She gave talks to several work groups in our facility, and we began to realize that the people from the other firm were not bad people. We began to realize that we were all in this thing together."

MANAGERIAL SUCCESS POINTERS
Achieving Success Amidst Mergers and Acquisitions

➤ Make a conscious decision to communicate information about the M&A on a continual basis.

➤ Publicize anything the two firms are doing together.

➤ If possible, involve your employees in merger activities such as integration teams.

➤ Give your employees a chance to air their fears and provide counseling and social support.

➤ Treat those employees who leave with dignity.

Six

Working with
Diverse Co-Workers

The United States is highly diverse. Our society consists of people with many religions, many cultures, and many different roots: African, South American, Asian, European, Middle Eastern, and Indian.

In the past, the American work setting did not accurately reflect the diversity of our population, particularly in managerial positions. Today, for the first time in our history, white males constitute a minority, only 46 percent of our working population. This is the beginning of a major demographic change in our work force. Let's take a closer look at some interesting statistics:

- Today, African-Americans, Asian-Americans, and Hispanics constitute 21 percent of the American population. Over 30 percent of the residents of New York City are foreign born. The population of Detroit is about 63 percent African-American. San Francisco is about one third Asian-American, while Miami is about two thirds Hispanic.[1]
- By 1988, minorities will make up 25 percent of the U.S. population. By the year 2000, English will be the second language for the majority of Californians. By the year 2030, the majority of the state's entry-level employees will be Hispanic.[2]
- White males will constitute only 15 percent of the 25 million new entrants that join the work force by the year 2000. The remaining 85 percent will be mainly white females, immigrants, and minorities of African-American, Hispanic, and Asian-American origins.[3]

- By the year 2000, the Hispanic and Asian-American populations are each expected to grow by 48 percent, the African-American population by 28 percent, and the white population by only 5.6 percent.[4]
- By the year 2000, 51 percent of the total work force will be female.[5]
- Sometime during the next century, whites will become the minority in the U.S. population.[6]

What does all this mean? Quite simply, it means that we have to deal with increased diversity right now, and much more in the future. David Kearns, president and CEO of Xerox, makes the point powerfully: "It is absolutely clear that we have to manage diversity right now and much more so in the future. American business will not be able to survive if we don't have a large diverse work force, because those are the demographics — no choice! The company that gets out in front of managing diversity, in my opinion, will have a competitive edge."[7]

Unfortunately, many people in our society grew up with little or no contact with people from other cultures. The prospect of working with, or even managing, people who are different can cause apprehension. In this chapter, we talk about various things that you can do to achieve success in a multicultural work setting and not be scared doing it.

John's Story

John Holt recently took over as one of four area managers at a very large general retail store in south Chicago. It is part of a chain of sixty-three stores located throughout five Midwestern states, and sells a wide range of merchandise including groceries, apparel, furniture, hardware, housewares, sporting goods, and automotive supplies.

John's store is one of the largest in the chain. It employs close to 500 people. The work force is quite diverse, with a large number of women, African-Americans, Hispanics, Asian-Americans, older workers, and disabled persons. John is forty-eight years old; he is white.

About 70 percent of the employees work on a part-time basis, anywhere from fifteen to thirty hours per week. The store remains open for business twenty-four hours a day, every day of the year; each employee is assigned, in a two-week rotation, to one of three shifts: day, evening, or night.

The store is headed by Pat Lowry, the store director. Reporting directly to Pat are John and three other area managers, each responsible for one main segment of store operations: hardlines, softlines, grocery, and cashiering.

John is the hardlines area manager, which means he is responsible for everything in the store with the exception of groceries, clothing, and cashiering. Six of the store's eighteen department managers report directly to him: Juanita Alvarez (automotive), Roberta Rawles (sporting goods), Leslie Johnson (furniture), Pat Young (plumbing and electrical), Kim Park (hardware), and Jack Baugh (paint).

Before taking his current position, John was the hardlines area manager of a much smaller store in southern Indiana. The merchandise was similar, but the neighborhood was different. The old store was located in a middle-class, suburban area where most of the employees as well as most of the customers were, as John often stated, "similar to me." Now John is faced with a diverse group of department managers, hourly employees, and customers.

For the most part, John's new job is quite similar to his former position. He makes sure that all merchandise in his area is stocked adequately, shelved properly, displayed attractively, and priced correctly. He is also responsible for maintaining good customer relations and the effective handling of all personnel within his departments.

But the situation *feels* different, and John is nervous. He's concerned about working with employees and customers who are different from himself. He's never been in that situation before, and he's not sure if he'll be successful.

Strategies for Employees

We hear a lot about diversity these days, but what does it really mean? If you think of diversity as focusing on the hiring and promoting of women and minorities, you're not alone.

Here lies one of the major problems with the concept of diversity: most people don't understand what it really means. It is not a synonym for equal employment opportunity (EEO). Nor is it a code word for affirmative action (AA). There is nothing legal about it. It has nothing to do with your social responsibility or ethics. It says nothing about your company having to hire or promote a certain percentage of women and minorities.

Valuing diversity simply means understanding and valuing differences between yourself and others. The goal is to get people to understand that *all* individuals are different. Gender and race certainly contribute to differences between people, but they are merely *two* of the many factors that make up the unique individual.

Take a moment to think about the co-worker who is most like you; the two of you might be the same sex, race, and just about the same age. Then ask yourself in what ways you differ. If you take the time and give this question a lot of thought, you'll be surprised to see how many ways you are, in fact, different. For example, you might have different education, ethnic backgrounds, political views, religions, family values, styles of managing, ways of approaching problems, modes of handling stress, personality characteristics, or manner of dress.

This list could go on and on. The point is that no two individuals are exactly alike. We all differ from one another. Valuing diversity means recognizing and appreciating these differences.

Why should you even worry about diversity? For one thing, it can't be ignored any longer. Due to the changing demographics in the United States, differences among employees will continue to increase over the next few decades. For another thing, diversity is about making a profit and remaining competitive. It accomplishes this by fully tapping the human resource potential of every member of your company's work force.

Here's one example. A few years ago, an industrial plant in Alabama with a highly diverse work force was threatened with closing unless its productivity improved. To save their jobs, everyone pitched in and achieved the production levels that were needed to stay in business — *everyone!* The division and plant managers were flabbergasted. For years, they had thought women, minorities, and disabled workers belonged only in lower-level jobs, where they were expected to do their jobs but no more. This crisis gave these managers a glimpse of what can happen when everyone works up to their true potential. Here's what the plant manager told us: "I can now see that we weren't getting from certain segments of our work force what they were really capable of giving."

It's important to remember this: the laws governing EEO and AA are based on the notion that people are more similar than they are different. Consequently, employees should be treated in the same way, no matter what groups they belong to or what their special concerns are. In contrast, valuing diversity means that people are appreciated for being different. In the workplace where diversity is a value, all are encouraged to be conscious of a wide range of differences (native language, national origin, age, sexual preference, work style) between themselves and their co-workers.

There are those who contend that the idea behind EEO and AA was to minimize differences and expect everyone to fit comfortably into the dominant culture. This new notion of diversity doesn't attempt to deny or deemphasize differences among people.

John Holt has decided that one of the major advantages of having a diverse group of department managers and employees is that they will bring a whole new set of ideas to his store. John realizes that, in order to compete successfully in today's dog-eat-dog retail business, new ideas are essential.

Understand Your Own Values and Prejudices

Before you can deal constructively with others who are different from you, you will need to become fully aware of your values and prejudices, things you have heard and believed all your life. People who say things like, "Hey, I'm a liberal, I'm not prejudiced" often hold on to more prejudices than they realize. They could use help in learning to understand themselves better.

The best method of self-exploration is to keep a log of

your major activities, work-related and otherwise, over several weeks. At the end of the period, review your log and ask yourself two basic questions:

1.   Where do I spend most of my time?
2.   What does it tell me and others about what I value and believe?

To gain greater insight into yourself, you need to ask and answer two additional questions:

3.   What significant emotional events have occurred in my life that have contributed to my values and attitudes about diversity?
4.   What do I need to do to improve my personal effectiveness in working with people culturally different from me?

John has done quite a bit of self-examination. He realizes that both he and his wife, Kathryn, have had no significant emotional events in their pasts involving African-Americans, Hispanics, or Asian-Americans. All they know is what they've read through the years in newspapers and magazines and seen on television. John and Kathryn agree that now they feel uncertain and vague. They have concluded that, now that they're living and working near Chicago, they need to make the effort to get to know people who are different from them.

No Special Treatment

When their organizations make a commitment to valuing diversity, many people react negatively. Two things in particular worry them: that performance standards will drop, and that minorities and women will get special treatment.

Let's dispel these two misconceptions right here and now. No one in business today expects employers to lower their standards in order to accommodate diversity. Diversity does not mean tolerating mediocrity. In fact, just the opposite is true; competence counts more than ever. Diversity means getting from each and every employee everything that they have to offer. As R. Roosevelt Thomas, Jr., executive director of the American Institute for Managing Diversity at Morehouse College in Atlanta, puts it: "If the old homogeneous work force performed dependably at 80 percent of its capacity, then the first result means getting 80 percent from the new heterogeneous work force too. But the second result, the icing on the cake, the unexpected upside that diversity can perhaps give as a bonus, means 85 to 90 percent from everyone in the organization."[8]

Are you wondering why a heterogeneous work force can be expected to be more productive than a homogeneous one? The answer is simple. The quality of decisions improves dramatically when made by diverse work groups. The reason is that these groups do not suffer from "groupthink." Groupthink typically occurs when a group of like-minded people work together. They become deeply involved in their cohesive group, and their desire to protect this cohesiveness overrides any attempts to realistically appraise alternatives, causing a deterioration in the group's decision-making ability. On the other hand, the diverse group may take longer to arrive at a decision, because of healthy disagreement, but the quality of the final decision will be higher. Individuals in a diverse group haven't had the same past experiences, don't think the same way, and therefore, don't come up with the same solutions.

John has already noticed that at the new store, his weekly area meetings with the department managers run longer than at his other store. There's a lot more discussion and disagreement among the seven of them, but he's quite pleased with the calibre of the business decisions made.

If the work force is diverse, management can be expected to eliminate or reduce any problems that affect minorities or women, but not to give them special advantages over other employees. Likewise, management can be expected to take steps to include all employees in both the formal and informal activities of the work group, but not to give minorities or women special protections against normal work standards, discipline, or termination unless they were given to all employees.

Be Careful of Your Assumptions

Consider this scenario: a white male manager walks through the office and passes two Hispanic men talking at the watercooler. He wonders why are they standing there wasting time. A few minutes later he sees two women coming out of the ladies room and chatting. He wonders what trivial issue they are gossiping about and hopes they get back to work quickly. He also observes two white males talking, one sitting on the edge of his desk, the other leaning against the office wall. What are his managerial assumptions? The Hispanics and women are wasting time; the white men are discussing business.

Since the manager hasn't really heard their conversations, he doesn't realize that the Hispanics and the women were talking business while the white males happened to be talking about their children. His misinterpretation of what he saw merely reinforces his bias that Hispanics and women don't work hard enough.

Stereotypes are always bad because they prevent differentiated thinking about people who belong to the stereotyped group. Stereotypes are typically invalid and they cause us to make inaccurate assumptions about other individuals who belong to a certain group. Stereotyping is the opposite of valuing diversity. Rather than viewing each person as an individual, it lumps co-workers into convenient, but inaccurate, pigeonholes.

What should you do to guard against making false assumptions about others? First of all, stop walking on thin ice. So many people are afraid they might sound prejudiced if they dare to mention any sort of difference between themselves and a co-worker. Pretending that differences are nonexistent can be damaging because it prevents what is natural: curiosity, informality, and openness. Cultural differences between ourselves and others, if handled tactfully and at an appropriate time, are legitimate items for conversation. When you do this, you'll feel better and so will the other person. You'll learn, for instance, that this individual is proud of his Cherokee, African, Jewish, Mexican, or Arab heritage and appreciates that you're interested in finding out more about it. However, be prepared to have some dearly held assumptions splattered! The worst thing that could happen is that the person doesn't want to discuss it with you. If so, then politely drop it.

Second, put your old assumptions to the test. When you find that a co-worker fits your stereotype, that's when you have to analyze all your assumptions.

There is an electrician at John's store who is originally from South Korea. Lee is quiet, hard-working, and very proud of his education and technical expertise. He enjoys working alone and rarely speaks up during meetings. He volunteers to help the other maintenance employees only when they ask for assistance; when he does help them, he does an outstanding job.

Lee has applied several times for promotion into management, but he keeps getting turned down. John and other managers in the store have concluded that Lee is an excellent technician, but that he lacks management skills. Perhaps they think managers have to be more assertive than Lee is. In fact, John is unaware of the fact that Lee has successfully, in his own quiet manner, helped to lead many of his group's maintenance projects for some time.

Recently, John has had to observe Lee's performance for himself. John realizes that in a diverse work force he must learn new ways to recognize managerial talent. After putting aside his stereotypes and looking at Lee's actual work, John realized that he and other managers had made wrong assumptions. Lee finally got promoted and has been doing a great job of handling the installation of lighting in the store's building expansion.

Guard Against the Similar-to-Me Effect

Most of us prefer to socialize with people who are like ourselves. We also have a better opinion of them. Research has shown conclusively that people have a tendency to like and to think more favorably of other people whom they perceive as being similar to themselves.[9]

It is flattering and reinforcing to find others who are similar to us. Don't you have friends who tend to have the same values and attitudes about things as you do? This is permissible in our private lives; we certainly are free to select friends with whom we feel comfortable. It becomes a problem at work when we tend to like only those co-workers who are similar to us, disliking and fearing co-workers who are somehow different.

Even worse is getting into what S. Kanu Kogod calls a "cultural collision," some conflict with a co-worker who is very dissimilar.[10] If it happens, here are the four things that you will need to do to improve this uncomfortable situation:

1. *Listen.* Actively listen to what the other person has to say and then respond to *what* was said, not *how* it was said or the style in which it was said.
2. *Diagnose.* Determine together the cause(s) of the problem. Is it due to miscommunications, misperceptions, intrusion from a third party, or differences in your job expectations?
3. *Generate options.* Together come up with some potential solutions that don't cause harm or a loss in dignity to either of you.
4. *Problem solve.* Work together to find the best solution, and then determine what actions each of you has to take to make it happen.

Fortunately, John is well aware of the similar-to-me effect, and he is making a conscious effort to guard against his natural tendency to "flock together" with Leslie Johnson and Jack Baugh. They are quite similar to him in terms of basic values, political attitudes, and background; what's more, all three men enjoy playing golf and tennis, attend the same church, and live in the same area of the city. The same can't be said of Juanita Alvarez, Roberta Rawles, Kim Park, and Pat Young.

Much to John's credit, he recently avoided a cultural collision with Juanita. John was upset with the way she had handled a customer who allegedly shoplifted some automotive wax from her department. Juanita refused to listen to the customer's side of the story, lost her temper, and accused him of being a thief. Soon after hearing about what happened, John met privately with Juanita and listened to her side of the story. Together, they diagnosed why she handled the situation as she did and what she should do differently in the future.

Beware of the Halo Effect

Have you ever noticed that when you have a strong negative opinion about a co-worker, you tend to act as though this person cannot do anything right? In actuality, he may possess only one or two characteristics that you don't like, but somehow these characteristics spread to the point where there's nothing you like about him. We call this a negative halo.

The opposite can occur as well. An individual possesses only a few characteristics that you like, yet you allow these few things to color your overall impression of this person so that the person can do no wrong—a positive halo. In most cases, a halo causes a judgment error about another person. After all, few people are either all good or all bad. Reality, in most cases, lies somewhere in between.

If you feel that you've fallen victim to either a negative or positive halo, simply sit down and force yourself to describe this individual in great detail. Write down all your thoughts about this person, and get opinions from others—those who seem to like the person and those who don't. When you've finished, here's what you're going to find: a realistic combination of strengths and weaknesses. After doing this easy exercise, you are going to be able to work with this individual in a healthier and more productive manner in the future.

John thinks that Roberta Rawles, manager of sporting goods, can't do anything right as a manager. After writing down *all* his thoughts about Roberta (her managerial limitations and her strengths) and seeking others' opinions about her, John realizes that he has fallen victim to negative halo effect. John now sees that Roberta has quite a few managerial assets that he hadn't given her credit for. He now realizes that one characteristic—she is closed to new ideas—bothered him greatly and spilled over into his opinion of her in other areas.

Identify Barriers

Cultural diversity has many advantages for you and your organization, but there's no denying it brings a new set of problems. In light of this, it's a good idea to get together with your co-workers in a group setting to brainstorm the diversity-related barriers you face in trying to accomplish your work.

Recently we attended a meeting of this type. Two groups—we'll call them the X's and O's—discovered these roadblocks existed:

- The X's feel that the O's haven't demonstrated the same level of expertise as they have. The O's think that they have and are insulted that the X's feel this way.
- The X's want to work solely with X's; O's are willing to work with X's, but don't have the opportunity.
- The O's feel that the X's are favored by management and get the choice work assignments.

Identifying these diversity-related barriers is only half the battle. The other half involves working together to find ways to overcome them. In this example, the group decided to pair up X's and O's. They felt that this demonstrated to the X's that the O's were equally competent technically, helped the O's get into the X network, and equalized the choice assignments across subgroups.

John's six department managers agreed to meet as a group to find out if there are any diversity-related barriers affecting store productivity. They learned that Juanita and Roberta feel that their ideas have often been ignored in staff meetings. The two women pointed out that the other department managers — all men — frequently cut them off when they're expressing their ideas and opinions. Everybody agreed that they would stop doing this to Juanita and Roberta, and Juanita and Roberta agreed that they needed to work on being more assertive when they are ignored or interrupted.

Strategies for Managers

If you as a manager are to support diversity in your organization, what do you need to do? First, here's what you should *not* do: ignore (or pretend to ignore) individual differences. When a manager says, "I didn't even notice that she was Japanese," what that manager is really communicating to the employee is, "The difference between us is not important to me; I see you as being just like me." It is just as bad to completely ignore differences as it is to emphasize them day after day. Managing at either extreme will cause problems.

In some multicultural workplaces, many different types of

EMPLOYEE SUCCESS POINTERS
Achieving Success in an
Increasingly Diverse Work Force

➤ Rethink the notion of diversity.

➤ Work on becoming more aware of your own values and prejudices.

➤ Remember that diversity does not mean lowering performance standards or preferential treatment for minorities and women.

➤ Keep in mind that a more diverse work force can lead to an increase in productivity.

➤ Eliminate inaccurate stereotypes by putting them to the test.

➤ Beware of falling victim to the similar-to-me effect.

➤ Be careful not to commit halo error.

➤ Identify any diversity-related barriers in your work group, and discuss ways to overcome them.

---

employees may be working side by side. Managers in these settings are understandably confused. Many ask, "How can I possibly learn about and react to all of these different cultures without becoming a nervous wreck?"

Of course you can't possibly learn everything about the many cultural differences and preferences among your employees. But the more you learn, the better able you will be to handle a diverse work group. The key point is to see people for who they are.

Second, take the time to understand your own culture. Many whites, especially those of European heritage, make the mistake of thinking they don't even have a culture. They think of "culture" as something that only minority group members have.

Finally, don't think you have to walk on eggs around your

employees. Openly and tactfully, talk with them about their unique cultures, and incorporate this information into your management practices.

Let's look at some of the other things that managers need to know to facilitate diversity within their organizational units.

Motivation: Different Strokes for Different Folks

Most management best-sellers that give advice on how to motivate people are based on the implicit assumption of a homogeneous white male work force. In fact, the most widely espoused theories of employee motivation reflect the white male's own experiences and attitudes. Some of these methods can be counterproductive when applied to women, African-Americans, Chicanos, Hispanics, Asian-Americans, or native Americans. Let's look at a few examples of how this happened in John's store:

• One of the department managers was excited with the work performed on a project by one of his employees, a native American. The manager decided to reward him with a lot of fanfare and congratulations in front of his peers, just as the management books suggest. Feeling uncomfortable with public attention, especially with his native American friends, this employee didn't come to work for several days.

• Another manager likes to recognize the accomplishments of his salespeople by occasionally giving them a pat on the arm or back. His Asian-American employees, who abhor being touched, avoid him like the plague. Two of them are so uncomfortable with the touching that they even asked for transfers to another department.

• Fresh from a course on effective managing, a manager learned that delegating responsibility can be quite motivating to employees. Therefore, she asked her primarily Filipino staff to alert her to any problems they might be experiencing with some new warehouse equipment. Instead, they used every possible makeshift remedy. Having to inform the supervisor of their inability to handle certain equipment problems would mean losing face.

Some managers think that it's a mistake to say that employees have different needs based on their cultural backgrounds. Avon's director of multicultural planning and design, Daisy Chin-Lor, eloquently counters this erroneous way of thinking: "If I were planting a garden and wanted to have a number of flowers, I would never give every flower the same amount of sun, the same amount of water, and the same soil. I'd be sure to cultivate each individual type of flower differently. Does that mean that the rose or the orchid is less because I have to do more with them? Certainly not!"[11]

Before joining Apple Computer in 1987 as vice president of human resources, Kevin Sullivan worked at Digital Equipment Corporation, where over 40 percent of the sales force were women and minorities. Sullivan says that many of the managers at Digital, back in 1987, believed that women and minorities were motivated in the same ways as white males. The results of an attitude survey, however, convinced them that there were dramatic differences. For instance, at the end of a sales meeting, the men would all go to a bar where they would get some "real feedback"; the women felt uncomfortable doing this. Sales meetings were usually held at a posh country club, but quite a few of the minority salespeople didn't attend because they didn't feel welcome. Sullivan pointed out that a manager at Digital, sensitive to the issue of cultural diversity, came up with a solution that worked: breakfast meetings at hotels in areas where everyone felt comfortable.[12]

Commitment from the Top

For diversity to truly be valued in any organization, there must be a significant level of senior management support — real commitment, not simply passive toleration. Let's look at some of the things top-level management at leading companies are doing to foster diversity:

- At Honeywell, special interest groups for women employees and minority employees meet to discuss their concerns and make recommendations for change. Many top-level executives work closely with these groups, providing not only resources but also their leadership skills and executive-level sponsorship.[13]

- At McDonald's, top-level executives were the first to attend management development programs that view diversity from a value-added viewpoint. The company believes that unless upper-level managers really understand what diversity is and how it benefits individuals and the organization, there's not much sense in taking the time to expose lower-level employees to this kind of training.[14]

- At Philip Morris, senior executives and minority representatives participate together on task forces that monitor organizational policy and practices for evidence of unfairness.[15]

- At Procter & Gamble, upper management not only talks up the advantages of having a diverse work force, but models it as well: about one-third of its managers are women and minorities.[16]

- Avon's successes with diversity started with upper management's support in the earliest stages. Avon's chairman and chief executive officer played a key role in establishing the program's tone while he was still executive vice president. The company's minorities and women's participation council includes the CEO, division presidents, top-level human resource people, and legal personnel. The council has been looking into how the company's corporate culture might be hindering the upward mobility of women and minorities, and suggesting ways to change that environment.[17]

Talk Up Those Unwritten Rules

Unwritten rules for getting ahead are a fact of life in any organization. These rules are never written down in black and white, yet they have a large impact on one's career success within the organization. Some examples are:

- How bosses and employees are supposed to relate to one another during business meetings. For example, how strongly can employees disagree with their managers?
- Whether higher-level managers should be addressed formally or informally.
- Appropriate dress at corporate headquarters.
- Who should socialize with whom away from work.
- How formal or informal an employee should be when making presentations at meetings.

Most white males know the rules; they've been playing by them since they were young. In fact, they created the rules: in most organizations they are in control and therefore they call the shots. One of your most important responsibilities as a manager is to make sure that the employees who don't know these rules hear about them.

That doesn't mean that all employees must slavishly follow all the rules all the time. Clearly, conforming to these unwritten rules stifles individuality—the very opposite of what valuing diversity is all about. Nevertheless, if employees want to be successful within an organization's milieu, some degree of conformity is appropriate. Your job as a manager is to help each employee fit into the organization culture and not get derailed, without having to give up cultural individuality.

In a few weeks, Kim Park is going to make a presentation to Pat Lowry and several other store directors from the company's five Chicago-area stores. John believes that Kim has a tendency to do two things that can hurt the effectiveness of his presentation and hence his reputation within the company: he presents too many facts and figures, and he responds to many questions by saying, "I'm sorry, I can't answer that until I collect more data." John decides to take Kim aside and suggest that he go easy on the numbers and answer questions as best he can with the data he's already gathered. After Kim prepares his presentation, John asks to hear it. He is able to give Kim constructive feedback before the actual presentation.

Training Is a Must

It's not enough to bring large numbers of people from diverse backgrounds into your company and assume that everything will work out. Few of today's managers and supervisors have the skills needed to manage diversity effectively. They may have attended management development programs focusing on such skills as delegation and time management, but few have received any training in managing diversity.

Training is a must! It should accomplish two basic objectives: raising awareness and building skills.

Training designed to achieve the first objective should explain the meaning of diversity, introduce the topic of managing diversity, and include information on work-force demographics. It should also involve some experiential exercises designed to get the managers thinking about relevant issues and raising their own self-awareness.

Ford Motor Company offers a three-day training session for managers and supervisors called "Managing Personnel Diversity." It is used to bring about a clearer understanding of the responsibilities of managing a diverse work force and a better appreciation of the values that diversity brings. Starting in the late 1980s, 3M added a module on managing diversity to its regular supervisory development program. During this module, 3M supervisors explore what it means to manage people of diverse backgrounds. Hewlett-Packard, at its manufacturing plant in San Diego, helps Americans better understand the differences in communication styles between themselves and Mexicans, Filipinos, and Indochinese.[18]

The skill-building training should focus on giving managers and supervisors help in managing and developing a work force that is much different from what they've been used to. Among the companies that have made extensive use of this training are Tenneco, Ortho Pharmaceuticals, Digital Equipment, Exxon, the World Bank, and the Internal Revenue Service.

Some of the essential behaviors that any skill-building training should emphasize include:

- To get respect, you have to give respect. Treat people as you would want to be treated.
- Be a mentor. Share yourself—your ideas, your knowledge, and your experiences. Don't hold back.
- Take a strong stand with employees of your own sex, race, or ethnic background by letting them know that cultural stereotyping is destructive.
- Avoid showing favoritism of any type.
- Don't allow cliques to form. If they start, get in and break them up.
- Create an atmosphere where problems among employees can be discussed openly and solved rationally.
- Show your employees that you're genuinely interested in learning more about their cultural backgrounds.
- Promote a work environment that is culturally friendly by not stereotyping or making assumptions about cultures.

Fortunately for John, his company provided a four-part training program known as Enjoying Diversity. It raised his awareness about diversity issues and helped him develop his managerial skills within this type of environment. More than anything, John has learned how to respect his employees, his department managers, and his customers. In turn, they respect him more.

This diversity training has also helped John to break up cliques that were starting to form among his six department managers. Jack Baugh and Leslie Johnson constituted one clique; Juanita Alvarez, Roberta Rawlers, Pat Young, and Kim Park constituted another. By giving a special assignment that required the input and cooperation from all six department managers, John was able to head off this problem.

Don't Fall Victim to Communication Problems

Much of the misunderstandings among diverse groups stems from their different styles of communicating. Let's take a look at a few common examples of miscommunication:

1. A female staffer takes an idea to her male boss. "The way I see it," she says, "I think that we could increase productivity by making these scheduling changes. In my opinion, it would be a good idea." Her manager responds by asking her to go back and do more research.
2. You're explaining the new inventory system to an African-American employee. His eyes keep wandering away from you.
3. A Hispanic employee tells you about a machine problem that she's having. Rather than getting directly to the point, she goes off on tangents. She also seems very emotional.

If you aren't knowledgeable about differences in communication styles across groups, you would assume that the first woman wasn't confident in her idea because she used so many qualifiers: "the way I see it," "I think," and "in my opinion." You would also assume that the man who didn't look you in the eye wasn't interested and wasn't listening. And you would assume that the second woman was not organized and clear in her thinking and much too emotional.

All three assumptions are incorrect. Women typically use more qualifiers than men, African-Americans often have less eye contact when listening than whites, and Hispanics usually take longer to get to the point and display more emotion when they speak.[19]

Unless You Manage Diversity, It Will Manage You

Diversity is a fact of life. Whether you like it or not, it's here to stay. If you don't learn to manage it, it will manage you.
Here are some of the things you might consider doing:

• *Orientation.* Some companies have special orientation sessions for new women and minority employees and their managers. Procter & Gamble has a program called "On Boarding."[20]

• *Language training.* Organizations with a multicultural work force, recognizing that languages other than English are

---

MANAGERIAL SUCCESS POINTERS
Achieving Success in an
Increasingly Diverse Work Force

➤ Don't be blind to individual differences that exist among your employees.

➤ Work on understanding your own culture.

➤ Discuss openly and tactfully each employee's culture and incorporate this information into how you go about managing and motivating that person.

➤ For diversity to be truly valued in any organization, senior-level management needs to support it, not just tolerate it passively. Help this to happen.

➤ Make certain that your employees who don't know the unwritten rules of getting ahead learn about them from you.

➤ Make sure that you and other managers receive training in managing a diverse work force.

➤ Strive to better understand the differences in communication styles between different cultural groups.

➤ Most of all, remember this: the best way to get respect is to give respect.

---

important, offer second-language training to both Anglos and minority-culture employees. Economy Color Card, Esprit De Corp., and Pace Foods are among them.[21]

• *Flexible work environments and benefits.* Organizations can promote diversity by making the work climate more flexible and tolerant of different cultures and life-styles. Two that are doing so are Patagonia and Hewlett-Packard.

Patagonia, based in Ventura, California, manufactures

products for active outdoor enthusiasts. It has about 450 employees, 40 percent of whom are in their twenties. In its nontraditional office environment, there are no offices, everyone works in open spaces, there are flexible work hours, and employees have the option of working at the office for five hours a day and at home for three hours. This accommodates many of the needs of the "twentysomething" generation.[22]

The work environment at Hewlett-Packard (HP) is beneficial to people from nontraditional cultural backgrounds because their approaches to solving problems at work are frequently different. HP encourages informality, unstructured work, loose supervision, and objectives set in broad terms with a lot of individual discretion regarding how they are to be achieved. Many other companies such as Levi Strauss, Arthur Andersen, and IBM have made important changes in benefits such as child care, parental leave, part-time work, and leaves of absence.[23] These companies have taken steps to help employees with differing needs be a successful part of the work force.

• *Performance appraisal and reward systems.* It's simple — people do what they are reinforced for doing. Organizations such as Baxter Health Care, Exxon, Amtrak, and Coca-Cola tie compensations and promotions to managers' performance in diversity efforts, such as mentoring females and minorities.[24]

• *Error reduction training.* Diversity won't thrive in an organization where managers and employees fall victim to errors of judgment such as stereotyping, similarity/dissimilarity error, first impressions, halo, and comparison (contrast). People must learn to see one another accurately. Many companies, including General Motors, Ohio Edison, Allstate Insurance, Bridgestone Tire, and B. F. Goodrich, provide their managers with a program called "Avoiding Rating Errors," a half-day experiential training session that has been shown to successfully eliminate these errors.[25]

• *Identifying managerial talent.* Many organizations, among them Mobil Oil, IBM, McDonald's, Xerox, and Pepsico, have special programs to spot women and minorities with potential for senior management positions early in their careers.

SEVEN

Making the Most of
an Overseas Assignment

How would you go about giving performance feedback to Moroccan workers? How would you make an effective sales presentation to businesspeople in Taiwan? How would you negotiate a new labor contract with union leaders in Germany? Should you try to implement individual pay incentives in a Swedish glass factory? Can an American female reporting directly to a Japanese manager disagree openly with her boss?

These questions and many others like them are typical of the intercultural situations that American workers find themselves facing in this new era of globalization. Cultural interactions such as these have become more and more commonplace in the last fifteen years, as the number of multinational corporations and American companies doing business throughout the world has increased rapidly.

The first multinational corporation (MNC) in the United States goes back to the 1860s — Singer Sewing Machine. Today, there are more than 3,500 MNCs, 30,000 exporting manufacturers, 25,000 companies with overseas branches and affiliates, and 40,000 firms operating abroad on an ad hoc basis.[1] These companies are involved in such activities as manufacturing automobiles, drilling oil, selling farm equipment, renting hotel rooms, building factories, and producing pharmaceuticals.[2] Most of the world's MNCs are quite large and many of them are U.S. companies. For instance, six of the ten largest firms in the world (in sales) are American companies:[3]

1. General Motors (U.S.)
2. Royal Dutch Shell (Netherlands)
3. Exxon (U.S.)
4. Ford (U.S.)
5. IBM (U.S.)
6. Toyota (Japan)
7. IRI (Italy)
8. British Petroleum (Britain)
9. Mobil (U.S.)
10. General Electric (U.S.)

Coca-Cola markets worldwide, Arthur Andersen offers a global accountancy, Weyerhaeuser Company produces newsprint paper for overseas sales, Universal Medical Supply sells disposable syringes internationally, and Procter & Gamble has created a universal market for many of its household products.

Although most U.S. international businesses operate in Europe, more and more of them are appearing in the OPEC nations in the Middle East, as well as in Africa, Asia, and Latin America. Most of the American companies rely primarily on personnel from the host country, but they also bring in people from the United States.

This chapter focuses primarily on the Americans who are asked by their organizations to take a temporary overseas assignment, usually from three to five years. We often refer to these individuals as "expatriates."

A recent survey of executives employed at the *Business Week 1000* companies suggests that, in most MNCs, a stint abroad is becoming a valuable step in the corporate climb.[4] But many people find it difficult to succeed. The changes that they and their families experience overseas are often too much to bear. Various companies report that 16 to 40 percent of their expatriate employees choose to return from their assignments early, and each premature return costs their firm roughly $100,000.[5] Another 30 to 50 percent choose to remain in their international assignments, but are considered to be ineffective or marginally effective. What's more, the compensation package of these ineffective or marginally effective employees is high — about $250,000 per year.[6]

American companies must share some of the blame for this failure rate. A recent survey of 1,500 top managers worldwide, designed by Columbia University's business school, revealed that American executives are too parochial and insular. The survey faulted American managers for minimizing the importance of learning foreign languages and cultures, in contrast to executives from other countries. The research projected economic conditions to the year 2000 and predicted a shortage of talented American executives able to run global businesses.[7]

Chris's Story

Chris Evans is employed by a large, American, multinational electronics company with overseas operations in twenty countries. He has worked for this company for the past sixteen years, always in the company's facilities in the Southwest. Chris is currently an engineering manager at a plant in a small town in New Mexico. He and his family have made many friends there over the years, and they are very active in community activities.

Last week, Chris's manager, Karen, asked him if he would be interested in a three-year overseas assignment in Kyoto, Japan. If he is interested, she will arrange an interview with the overseas plant manager, Mr. P. W. Fugita, who is currently in the United States to put together a management team that will upgrade the quality and productivity of various products manufactured at the Kyoto plant. If Chris is selected, he would be a project coordinator in charge of rearranging floor space, changing machinery, and modifying production processes. He would have about twenty-five engineers and production specialists reporting to him; Chris himself would report to Mr. Fugita and represent his professional staff to the entire management team.

When Karen first mentioned this overseas assignment, Chris felt mixed emotions. On the one hand, he was excited; he knew this could be a very important career opportunity for him. He had always had his sights set on someday moving into middle-level management, but he had been passed over several times in the last few years. On the other hand, Chris is nervous. He has never traveled outside the country, nor even much beyond the Southwest. Chris and his family have always lived in small towns; would they be comfortable in a big city?

Chris and his wife Julie have two children: Mike, in his first year of high school, and Lindsay, who is in the second grade. Mike has a learning disability, and his grades have been weak in the past; recently, thanks to a special education teacher, he seems to be overcoming his problem. Julie is employed full-time as an accountant in a small CPA firm in their town. She returned to college in her early thirties, and has been with the firm since she graduated three years ago.

Chris knows that this position is his if he wants it. He has to let Mr. Fugita know his decision by the end of the week.

Strategies for Employees

Chris is wise to be concerned. The experience of living and working in a foreign country presents many challenges to American employees and their families. Here we look at some of the ways Chris — and you — can make this great adventure a career success, starting with making an informed decision. Throughout this section, comments from real people who have lived and worked abroad are included.

Making the Right Decision

It's flattering to be offered an overseas assignment, but it's a mistake to accept immediately, without thinking through what it might mean to your career and to your personal life with your family. So before you say yes, take the time to do your homework:

1.   Learn about yourself.
2.   Learn about the country.
3.   Learn about your job there.
4.   Learn about company policies for expatriates.

Do an Inner Search. Foreign assignments can mean an exciting adventure for the whole family and a significant boost for your career. They can also mean personal and professional disaster. As we have seen, more than one third of all expatriates return from their foreign services prematurely; many have damaged their careers and reputations within their companies. Some pay a terrible personal price in the form of divorce, alcoholism, or drug abuse.

Don't automatically assume that you will achieve success overseas just because you happen to be a successful manager or professional here at home. And don't automatically assume that because your company chose you, it's a good decision for you. Those who offered you this opportunity *may* have considered your qualifications quite carefully, but many companies are woefully weak in this area. The question of whether you have what it takes to succeed can best be answered by you. And that answer involves your family as much as it does yourself. You need to think carefully about these two questions:

1.   How do I feel about this? What do I see as the advantages and disadvantages to me personally?
2.   How is this going to affect my family — my spouse and my children?

Look inside yourself. Think about your personality, your working style. Be honest. Ask yourself:

> Are you flexible by nature?
> Can you adapt to new situations?
> Can you work without supervision?
> Do you have good interpersonal skills?

> "You've got to be able to handle increased responsibilities with less supervision and support. You're a long way from the home office. Technical advice isn't as available. At the same time, you've got to prove yourself all over again to these people. So, you've got to be independent, be able to achieve results with limited resources, and be a self-starter."

"You've got to be able to adapt your supervisory style to the culture. For instance, over there employees will do anything to avoid confrontation with a boss. If there's a problem, they'd do whatever you tell them to do and not question it. They'd also follow your instructions to the letter. So, when a problem existed, I couldn't be participative and get their input. I had to figure out how to solve the problem myself and then be careful to be very explicit and correct in my directions."

"You've got to be the kind of person who can develop good, friendly interpersonal relations with your host nationals. This makes it a lot easier to learn the intricacies and complexities of the new organization and culture."

Involve Your Family in the Decision. If members of your family are going with you to the new country, they should have an equal say in the decision. Even those who will remain at home have a part in the decision, for their lives are going to be affected. But certainly all those who will be expected to give up their familiar lives for the unfamiliar should have a vote.

"Nobody ever asked me if I wanted to go. I really didn't. I didn't want to leave our elderly parents for three years, not see our friends back home, and give up conveniences we're used to."

Spouses, particularly if they do not work outside the home, are under the greatest stress overseas. The employees at least have the everyday familiarity of their office and work.

"Your family must be able to cope successfully with the stresses of everyday life overseas. You also have to find ways to tolerate the stresses at work. Being stable and having a stable marriage and stable family is critical."

On the other hand, spouses who must give up their own job are often bitter.

> "I took a leave of absence from my law firm so Terry could have this career opportunity. I'm very sorry that I agreed to do this. I'm not working, I'm bored, and I miss home."

Let's not forget the problems that your children may experience. It's very difficult leaving their friends at home and having to adjust to new schools and new social groups. They also miss certain conveniences (fast-food restaurants, movies, TV, telephones) they're used to. Often the adjustment is toughest on teenagers, easiest for young children seven and under. But regardless of age, you must realize that this whole experience is tougher for your children than it might be for you. You have the continuity of the work environment. Your children, like your spouse, have to start over. It can be a strange and threatening experience, particularly making new friends, coping with new schools, and fitting in.

Remember, the overseas experience must be something you *want,* as opposed to feeling that you *must* do it for your career. And your family's feelings are critical. If your spouse or teenage children are opposed to leaving home, give them as much information about the positives and negatives. After that, if they are still strongly opposed, let the international transfer go, it will be more trouble than it's worth to you.

Twenty Questions. The twenty questions here can help you organize and focus your inner search. Take your time; think honestly about each one. Whenever you answer yes, move on to the next question. When the answer is "no," stop and focus on the reason or reasons why.

1. Am I accepting this overseas assignment simply to get away from domestic problems, either at work or at home?
2. Are my family and I really interested in learning about this particular country and its culture?

3. Are we the kind of family who will look at things over there in a very judgmental manner, always deciding something is "right" or "wrong"?

4. Are we the type of family who will be critical of things simply because they are at odds with our own value system and living habits?

5. Are we willing to learn the language before we leave and continue to learn it while we're overseas?

6. Am I willing to adapt my management style to fit the ways employees are typically supervised there?

7. Am I willing to experience a possible loss of authority and major functional responsibilities?

8. Are we willing to give up many of the conveniences that we currently enjoy?

9. Are we willing to give up activities that we now enjoy doing at home?

10. Will we be able to cope with various types of environmental difficulties, such as inadequate medical facilities, inferior educational institutions, climate discomforts, and lower living standards?

11. Do I have the emotional stability and flexibility to cope with the culture shock and stress?

12. Do my spouse and children have the emotional stability and flexibility to cope with the culture shock and stress?

13. Am I independent enough to stand on my own with little help or guidance from the home office?

14. Am I resilient enough to be able to bounce back when business things don't go my way?

15. Can my family and I laugh at ourselves when we're not in control of the situation and feel inept?

16. Will my family and I take advantage of this as a learning opportunity, and not just a business opportunity? Or, will we just kind of hole up with a bunker mentality?

17. Is our marriage stable enough to withstand whatever is in store for us abroad?

18. Do I possess the relational skills to get along well with co-workers and customers I will come in contact with overseas?

19. Do I have the technical expertise to handle this assignment?

20. Is this the right time for our family to be away from relatives and friends back home?

You don't have to have a perfect score to seriously consider accepting the assignment. But if you uncovered two or more areas of concern, you need to resolve these inhibitors or else decline the assignment.

Chris has done his inner search. The answers to questions 2, 3, 4, 5, and 20 concern him, because he's not sure whether this is the right time for his wife and his son to be away. Chris is also worried that perhaps he and his family are too "small town" to be able to adapt to a foreign culture. However, Chris knows that he's stagnating in his current position; gaining middle-level managerial experience abroad plus having the opportunity to be part of the management team interests him greatly. He believes that he himself has what it will take to be successful over there, and he's excited about the assignment.

Learn About Cultural Differences

You can't make a reasonable decision until you know what you're getting into. What does it really mean to live in a different culture, with different customs and values? To start with, you may have to adjust your way of thinking.

There is an enormous contrast between the cultures and basic value systems of the people of the United States and the remaining seven-eighths of the world. That doesn't mean that they're all "wrong" and only we Americans are "right." The values and customs of other cultures are not even "quaint"; they are as fundamental to people of those cultures and countries as yours are to you. Accepting the fact that cultural differences are legitimate is the first step.

> "You've got to have a willingness to accept the society, to adjust to it, rather than say it is wrong and our way is right. Things have to been seen as simply different, not wrong. Those of us who couldn't do this ended up associating only with other Americans.

They didn't learn much about the country's culture,
and they were unhappy."

The specifics will of course vary from one country to
another, maybe even one region to another, but in general cultural differences revolve around these fundamental values.

Change Versus Tradition. Our culture perceives change
as good. It is viewed as being synonymous with things we highly
value, such as creativity, growth, progress, and improvement.
In many other countries, change means a threat to what is valued — tradition, continuity, and stability. If one of your objectives is to initiate technological change, this value difference will
be keenly important. Expect resistance; prepare yourself for it.
You'll have to work on finding ways to make gradual changes
that are congruent with your host country's rich traditions.

Fate Versus Control. Most of the people of the world believe in the concept of fate; they believe that fate controls who
they are and what they are to do. They're also much more in-
clined to live harmoniously with nature and to accept it as it
is. Americans feel that we have a greater hand in controlling
our own destiny. We see problems as things we need to solve;
people of other cultures may see them as obstacles willed by God
that should not be meddled with. Don't be surprised if your host-
country employees resist your attempt to encourage them to set
monthly production goals. Don't waste effort agonizing over why
your co-workers don't see the value of the new nuclear power
plant that your company is building.

Equity Versus Status. Equity is one of our most important
values as Americans. We try to play down inequalities and to
emphasize equal opportunity for all. We like to think the "American Dream" is out there for anyone who wants to seek it. Other
cultures of the world view the concept of equality differently.
For them, such things as rank, status, and class differences make
sense because they provide security and certainty; people know
their proper roles and feel comfortable occupying them.

You need to be keenly aware of this value difference, especially if you're functioning abroad in a managerial position. In India, you may have subordinates who will bow as you pass them in the hallways. In the Philippines, your employees will save face at any cost. In Mexico, your employees might not inform you of problems that you need to know about simply because they value avoiding confrontation with their boss.

Informality Versus Formality. In many countries of the world, formality is the norm. Employees dress "properly" for work, people address one another by their titles and surnames, trainers instruct employees from behind podiums, and managers keep a great deal of psychological distance between themselves and those who report to them. Informality is disapproved in these cultures because it implies disrespect. On the other hand, in the United States we encourage leaders, managers, and employees to be informal and at ease in what could be formal situations. Employees address their managers on a first-name basis; everyone in a company uses the same parking lot and eating facilities.

Directiveness Versus Indirectiveness. A foreign associate described Americans as being "about as subtle as a barracuda." There's no doubt about it, our culture values directness and frankness. If we're having trouble with a co-worker, we like to try to talk directly and tactfully with that person. If we're asked to do something we're unable to do or don't want to, we are encouraged to say so. Other cultures may place a high premium on not confronting others for fear that the other person might lose face. Understanding your host country in this respect is quite important, for it will affect how you handle co-workers, employees, superiors, customers, and people in other companies.

Learn About the Country

You want to pick up as much information as you can about what it's *really* like to live and work in the host country. The best source for that kind of candid information is people who have been there.

Talk to Others Who Have Been There. Try to collect names of people who can give you both perspectives: the work situation and everyday life. Ask your co-workers if they know people in the organization who have served in the overseas office.

Contact the human resource people in your own division and your international personnel organization, and ask for names and phone numbers. At the same time, you and your family should be contacting neighbors, friends, co-workers, and acquaintances in the community. Find out who has worked or traveled to the country in question. Most of them will be more than willing to share their overseas experiences with you, either by phone or during a meal. It makes no difference whether they enjoyed their visit to the country or hated it. In either case, their experiences are invaluable to you.

You probably have lots of specific questions, but be sure not to overlook these:

1. What did you and your family derive out of living and working over there?
2. What things did you like least about living and working there?
3. Would you go back, and if you did what things would you do differently?

Spend Time in the Library. There is a rich source of free information: your public library. Some weekend afternoon, collect the family and make a trip. Send the teenagers to the video section to look for travel videos and to the music room for tapes; help younger children find children's books and stories about life in the host country. Among the adult books, investigate travel guides, historical novels, political and cultural guides. Browse through the periodicals room for relevant magazine articles; make a mental note of which magazines cover international events. Read a week's worth of newspapers from a major city in the host country.

In fact, once you begin thinking about the country, you will probably see material about it every time you turn around. Get in the habit of stopping at the largest magazine stand and checking the new issues of the magazines that you liked in the library.

We have to admire how much Chris has done to give himself a realistic country preview. Besides talking with neighbors and friends, he has gotten a lot of reading materials about his host country from the public library. He has contacted the public health service about inoculations, dietary restrictions, and sanitary data. He and his family have driven all the way to Dallas to go to ethnic restaurants, just to see whether they liked the country's food. While in Dallas, they went to the university and met with a few foreign students from the country.

Make a Preview Visit. If your company offers you and your family the opportunity to visit the country before your decision is final, by all means take advantage of it. In all likelihood the visit will be short, perhaps no more than a long weekend, so you will have to find ingenious ways to uncover the information that is of greatest concern to you and your family. Ask to see things like the neighborhoods where you might live, schools, places of worship, and stores. Look at what the stores generally stock. What community resources and amenities would be available to you and your family?

Chris and his family were given an all-expense-paid visit to their host country. All of them thought that it was interesting and beautiful and that the people were quite friendly. However, the country's culture deemphasized differences between people and therefore made no attempt to provide special help for students such as Mike. Mike mentioned that he would find it difficult in school without his teacher's help but that he'd do his best if his dad decided to take the overseas transfer. Chris and Julie discussed the fact that she wouldn't be able to work overseas and that she'd have to take some continuing education classes when the family returned. She expressed concern about not working and finding things to do to keep her occupied. But she also felt that this transfer would be an important stepping stone for Chris's career; if he really wanted it, she'd be willing to chance it.

Learn About the Job and Company Policies

Make sure you also find out in advance everything you can about the nature of the assignment. The person who is considering you for the overseas position should, of course, give you a complete briefing on what you will be doing, who you will report to, who will report to you — but unfortunately, that doesn't always happen. The point is, don't be shy about asking for the information. You don't want to end up like this person:

> "I didn't have the foggiest notion of my assignment. My boss at home couldn't help me. The people there were suspicious of me. They were not sure whether I was a spy from the home office or there to really help them."

And, since success depends in part on meeting expectations, be sure you are totally clear on the company's objectives in asking you to take this assignment? Do they want you to broaden your skills, take the skills you already possess and apply them to a particular business need, or give you the experience of working in another culture?

You also need to take responsibility for finding out the corporate policies on overseas assignments.

> What about medical coverage, housing, vacation time, and cost of living adjustments?
>
> What type of mentor arrangement will be provided during your assignment?
>
> What kind of repatriation plan does the company have?
>
> Who will look out for your interests while you're gone?
>
> What will your job be when you return?
>
> What support system will be provided to your spouse and/or children?

A useful support system for working abroad are other Americans from the same company who have lived in the foreign country. They are often able to take new expatriates under their wing and can show you the ropes. For example, many expatriates over time become acquainted with local people who can provide good medical care. Your colleagues abroad can introduce you to these people — or if they've returned to the United States, can provide referrals.

Chris met with Mr. Fugita and learned that the company was interested in broadening his technical skills and developing his managerial capabilities. Naturally, he liked hearing this. He also appreciated everything he heard about the company's policies and procedures, as well as several technical training programs that he would attend before leaving. Chris was distressed, however, when Mr. Fugita told him that, quite frankly, he hadn't thought about a mentor arrangement, a repatriation plan, support for Julie and the children, or what position Chris would occupy upon return.

Prepare for Success

You've decided to accept the opportunity. You've talked things over thoroughly with your family, gotten your job responsibilities clarified, and started a personal research program. Now you are ready to move right into the company's formal training program. If there is one.

Many companies with international operations offer comprehensive training programs in the culture, traditions, and everyday customs of the host countries. But many others do not. If your company does not have a formal program, brainstorm with your manager about other ways the organization can help you with training. Don't feel that you're being presumptuous. Remember, training will not only help you and your family, but will also help ensure your success, and therefore your company's success, abroad.

Language Training Is Critical. If nothing else, learn enough of the language so that you can at least understand and be understood at a basic level. Plan on a minimum of four weeks of language classes. Supplement your classroom experience by listening to audio cassettes or records in the foreign tongue. Read newspapers, magazines, or books in the new language. Try to speak to others who have this language skill, preferably native speakers, if possible.

"I was told I should try to learn a little Japanese, but that I'd be okay in Japan with English. I was

met at the Tokyo airport by someone who didn't
speak a word of English. Our stress level was out
of sight. Without a good command of the language,
our world was very limited. We came home six
months early."

How to Survive the First Six Months

You might as well know this in advance: the first six months
can be murder! Even with all your preparation, the culture shock
is still shocking. It seems that everything hits you at once: getting accustomed to the new office, moving into a new house,
getting the kids settled in school, and learning to cope with all
the thousands of details of daily life you never used to give a
second thought. The whole process can be very, very stressful.

> "We were never told that our whole personal life
> would be dependent on the company for the first
> couple of months. My husband's secretary had to
> go places with us. She even had to make a doctor's
> appointment for me. Nobody told us that we'd feel
> totally out of control."

Go Before Your Family. One way to relieve some of this
stress is to arrive a few weeks ahead of your family, if possible.
This will give you a chance to get acclimated and get some of
the basics under your belt, so you can help them with the early
adjustment.

> "My nine-year-old daughter came home from school
> soon after we had arrived. She was frantic and told
> us that she'd never go back to that place. This up-
> set my wife and our younger kids. I felt very badly
> at the time that I couldn't do much to alleviate
> everyone's pain because I was so stressed out start-
> ing my new assignment."

Also, try to arrange the schedule so that there are several
weeks of overlap between yourself and the person you are re-

placing. She can help you learn the ropes, both at work and in the community. She can even be your unofficial mentor, if no other person is slated for this role. Having this kind of backup when you first arrive will take the edge off the stress at work, leaving you with more emotional energy to help the family settle in.

If there's an American community in your host country, make certain to seek it out and become an active part. Just make sure you don't spend *all* your time there.

Keep Actively Learning. If you didn't learn the monetary system before you left home, that's one of the first things you'll need to do now. And you and your family will need to continue your language instruction so that you can all speak, understand, read, and write it proficiently.

> "You have to be willing to make a sincere effort to learn their language. Even if you're not successful and you make mistakes, they appreciate your effort. I'll never forget a sign at a hotel desk that sums up how they feel—'We don't speak English, but we won't laugh at your Spanish.'"

Get to know the people of your host country. Make every effort to understand their culture. Participate in cultural seminars conducted by the American Chamber of Commerce.

Generally speaking, the Americans who don't succeed are those who can't accept the fact that they are different and have different cultural values from their host nationals. What's more, they segregate themselves and associate only with fellow Americans. They go overseas and try to live exactly as they did at home. They not only make themselves miserable but also miss the wonders of living in another culture.

Take Measures to Deal with Stress. The first six months are usually harder on your family than they are on you. You at least can escape to the office—a somewhat familiar environment—five days a week.

"Your family has to spend about six tough months getting used to the new culture (schools, shopping, banking, phone installations) with very little help from you—the person responsible for their being there. I was fortunate; my family saw it as a challenge and learning experience. Even so, there were times when I felt they resented me because it was easier for me. I was immersed in my work during those initial months and didn't have to cope with their everyday frustrations."

You don't have to stand by and do nothing; there's a lot you can do to alleviate the stresses in your family. First, acknowledge the legitimacy of stresses that they are experiencing while you yourself are not. Second, encourage everyone to talk these stresses out. Call a family conference and brainstorm ways to minimize the stress—perhaps getting out of town for the weekend, going hiking or camping, attending a sporting event, getting a language tutor. In other words, you have to work as a family to find ways to cope.

And try to keep your sense of humor. It will get you through a lot of frustrating situations.

"You've got to be able to laugh at yourselves. Our family was basically illiterate in that we couldn't speak the language or even read the menu. In restaurants, we ordered by pointing to food at other tables or by taking the waitress outside and showing her a replica of what we wanted in the front window. Everyone chuckled, and we did too."

Look for the Sunshine. You have to go into this experience expecting changes and differences, and find ways to value them. In the United States, Chris and his family had a home in suburbia with a big lawn and a lot of space. Working in Kyoto involves living in an urban area with no yards and large crowds of people. Rather than getting upset with his lack of space, Chris looks at it from the point of view that he is within walking distance of lots of restaurants and interesting cultural sites and has the opportunity to explore new places. In the United States, Chris and his family were in the habit of getting in their car and driving anywhere. In Kyoto, traffic is terrible! Instead of complaining about the congestion, Chris learned to use public transportation. He soon realized it's an excellent system and a good way to feel that he's part of the culture.

Coming Back Home

If you think going was bad, coming home is even worse. This is cultural shock in reverse, and it's worse because it takes you by surprise: you don't *expect* to have trouble adjusting to your own home town. You expect things to be the same as when you left — and they're not. People expect you to be the same as you were before you left — and you're not.

> What things have changed in my organization, and how will these changes affect the position I will be returning to?
> What changes have occurred in American society since we've been gone, and what do we need to know and do to handle them?

Start getting ready for repatriation six months before your return. You will probably need to take it upon yourself to do this since most American companies don't provide formal reentry training. Actually, in a very real sense, you should start preparing for your reentry before you even leave home in the first place. You should find out in advance what position you'll have when you return; this should be part of your negotiation with your home managers. And from the earliest days of your time overseas, you should make plans to stay in touch.

Keep in Touch. Keep in touch with your home office while you're overseas, especially your manager and close co-workers. Write or telephone them periodically to learn what's happening. You might also keep in contact with the representative from the international personnel organization who interviewed you initially for the assignment.

> "I spent three years in South America. When I returned my whole division had been reorganized and I didn't know the new leaders. Their basic attitude seemed to be that I was on vacation for three years enjoying the sunshine while they were here busy working."

To keep current on American culture, buy American newspapers and magazines or have them mailed to you. If Cable News Network (CNN) is available, keeping up with events at home is a lot easier. In addition, periodic visits home are highly recommended. Most organizations allow you and your family to return home once a year. And be sure to stay in touch with friends and relatives during your stay.

> "So many things had changed at home while we were gone. We didn't know how to cope. For instance, we had no idea how to go about ordering telephones. All we wanted was a phone installed. Instead, we heard about three-way calling, call waiting, and buying our own phone. We felt like idiots."

> "We had one brand of orange juice in Mexico, if they happened to have it. When we returned, I found five different types of Minute Maid and fifty different types of cookies. I couldn't remember what brands we used to buy. I went home and cried."

Know What to Expect. Reentry adjustment is complex. Once again, your family is the key. Sit down as a family unit and acknowledge the changes that have occurred to each of you individually as well as all of you as a family. Recognize these changes, and get them out on the table. Unless you do this, you may not recognize how you've changed. This is what causes such personal difficulty.

In particular, you must be prepared for the changes in your perspective on your work. The sad truth is, many of your co-workers will not understand or even appreciate your experience.

> "My discontent started the first day I returned to work. Two of my colleagues asked me to tell them about it. I didn't realize till that moment how much I had learned about how our employees should be managed. I couldn't believe how much I had to say."

> "Before I left I was told to bring back new ideas. When I returned they acted as though I had never left. I changed a lot, but they treated me as though I hadn't. They really weren't interested in what I had learned overseas. This was a real letdown."

> "While I was over there, I developed an international business perspective. When I returned, I realized for the first time how parochial and narrow my co-workers are. They thought of themselves as merely a North American company."

One last point: be prepared for the fact that many people are not really interested in your experiences. Instead, they'll want to tell you about themselves.

> "My colleagues asked me to tell them about my experience, but all they wanted was a ten-second answer."

Strategies for Managers

In this area of international assignments, there is much to be done. American companies, by and large, have poor track records when it comes to training and supporting their employees during an overseas stint. In this section we look at some of the

---

EMPLOYEE SUCCESS POINTERS
Achieving Success in an International Environment

➤ Before accepting any international assignment, take the time to assess your own likelihood of success by asking yourself the twenty questions.

➤ Don't make the decision to accept an international assignment without discussing it with those family members who will be joining you.

➤ Make certain that you are aware of how American values differ from your future host country before accepting an assignment.

➤ Collect as much information about the country as possible. Talk with neighbors, friends, co-workers, and acquaintances. Spend time in the library. Make the most of your preview visit.

➤ Acquaint yourself with the company's policies about overseas assignments and its repatriation plan.

➤ Anticipate that the first six months will be a difficult period of adjustment for you and your family.

➤ Go into the experience expecting changes and differences, and find ways to value them.

➤ Prepare yourself ahead of time for the toughest part of working in an international environment: the reentry period.

---

things that managers can do to help their employees make a successful adjustment; often this may involve persuading senior management to set up systems where now there are none.

Improve the Selection Process

Although some organizations, such as IBM and Federal Express, do an outstanding job of selecting the right people to fill posts abroad, most do not. All too often American companies have relied on this faulty equation:

SUCCESSFUL DOMESTIC PERFORMANCE =
SUCCESSFUL OVERSEAS PERFORMANCE

This equation suggests that if an employee can produce within the United States, there is no reason why that employee's contribution would suffer if transferred to another country. If this were only true, selecting people to work overseas would be simple. The executive doing an excellent job in Cincinnati could be counted on to perform as well in Tokyo; the technically competent engineer in Schnectady, New York, would have no trouble being as effective in Hannover, Germany. Unfortunately, the selection process isn't that easy. If it were, our MNCs wouldn't be reporting that 40 percent of Americans selected for overseas assignments fail to function effectively in the foreign environment and choose to return from their tours early.[8]

Three hundred of the largest American MNCs were surveyed to find out *why* expatriates fail. The reasons, in descending order of importance, were[9]

1. The spouse's inability to adjust to a different physical or cultural environment
2. The employee's inability to adjust to a different environment
3. Other family-related problems
4. The employee's personality or emotional maturity
5. The employee's inability to cope with the larger responsibilities posed by overseas work
6. The employee's lack of technical competence for the job assignment
7. Lack of motivation to work overseas

Evaluate the Big Picture. Notice that of those seven reasons for failure, only two have to do with the employee's ability to do the job. All the rest concern personal traits and, most especially, the family's ability to cope. That's why the selection process must take into account more than simply the employee's technical competence.

Here are the four main areas that must also be assessed:

1. Ability to Relate
        Tolerance for ambiguity
        Adaptability
        Nonjudgmentalness
        Cultural empathy
        Interpersonal skills
2. Motivation
        Belief in the mission
        Congruence with career path
        Interest in overseas experience
        Interest in the specific host-country culture
        Willingness to acquire new patterns of behavior
        Willingness to acquire new attitudes
3. Family Situation
        Willingness of spouse and children to live abroad
        Adaptive and supportive spouse
        Stable marriage
4. Language Skills
        Host-country language
        Understanding of customs
        Understanding of subtle nonverbal communications

> "The individual and their spouse both have to see
> this as a desirable adventure in life. We've seen
> more failures because the spouse is unhappy than
> because the individual can't perform at work."

Use Good Selection Techniques. The attitude that domestic performance equals overseas performance may explain why
only 5 percent of companies administer psychological tests and
conduct in-depth interviews to determine the degree to which
candidates possess cross-cultural skills.[10] Instead, most companies continue to make costly mistakes by relying solely on interviewing the candidate and spouse at a superficial level. If psychological tests are used correctly to measure such things as
flexibility and interpersonal skills, they can be a valuable aid
in the final selection decision.

    Best of all would be a combination of three techniques —

in-depth interviewing, psychological testing, and the assessment center. American corporations have used assessment centers for years to make domestic hiring decisions. Candidates participate in group interactions designed to simulate actual situations that they might encounter on the job, and their reactions are observed by trained assessors. The assessors then rate each candidate on several behavioral dimensions such as leadership, interpersonal skills, behavioral flexibility, and stress tolerance. The beauty of the assessment center technique is that candidates are being judged not on their résumés or references but on how they actually *behave* in these simulated situations. The same technique can easily be applied to overseas selections; the situation would simply be set up to simulate the foreign experience.

Provide Complete Information

If you have chosen the person you want, and that person wants to go, don't think you're finished. The more information you can provide at this point, the more future problems you can head off.

Clarify the Job. The expatriate must be very clear about the nature of the overseas assignment. Go over the major job responsibilities and performance expectations in detail.

Explain Procedures. Take it upon yourself to learn the company's policies and procedures that relate to overseas service, and explain them to your employee in detail. This might involve such things as

> Medical coverage while overseas
> Paid vacations home
> Housing allowances
> Additional wages to compensate for increased cost of living
> Vacation, holidays, and paid travel
> Compensation for ongoing domestic expenses
> Education options for minor children
> Legal protections

One area that will be of great concern to the expatriate is the company's repatriation plan. When she returns to the United States after several years of foreign service, what will her position be? How will her seniority and promotion path be affected? If there is not a formal plan to cover these important areas, discuss with senior managers what you can do to protect your employee. This might trigger them to develop a formal plan covering all such situations. A repatriation plan should help protect the employee from

Loss of authority and discretion in decision making
Resentment among colleagues upon return
The feeling of isolation from domestic operations
The feeling that her company isn't capitalizing on the experience she earned overseas
Loss of visibility and contacts at headquarters
Culture shock

"An overseas assignment is now considered a good career alternative in our company. It wasn't always like this. Ten years ago it was a problem, but not now. You're now kept track of and never forgotten. Policy states that my performance must be reviewed each year. Also, at the end of my second year, the company must have a plan for my repatriation."

At the same time, you will also want to explain the company's mentor program and the family support systems that will be available; more about these a little later.

Fill the Information Vacuum. The person who is anticipating spending time in a foreign country usually knows how important it is to learn about that country ahead of time, but doesn't always know where to go.

The best thing you can do to help with this situation is put the candidate in touch with others in the organization who have worked and lived in the country; you are probably in a better position to request their names and phone numbers from the human resource department than the employee is.

If possible, these meetings should take place in their homes, rather than as a working lunch. And make it a family event, to promote a wide-ranging conversation.

Give the Family a Preview Trip. Send the whole family to the host country for a preview, all expenses paid. Actually, the ideal time to do this is while your main candidate is deciding whether to accept the assignment. But in any case, a preview trip is extremely helpful for long-term success. There are things about a country that one can learn only by direct observation, and knowing about them in advance can head off a lot of problems.

Make the preview as realistic as possible. A week's stay in London's Essex Hotel or the Ritz in Singapore doesn't realistically represent daily life in those two cities. Arrange for the employee and his family to stay in a rented apartment or house in the *actual* neighborhood where they will be living. Make sure they see the area's stores, schools, and recreational facilities. If possible, introduce them to some of the people in the neighborhood.

Provide Training and Support

Once you have made the investment in selecting the right person, do everything in your power to help that person be successful. Most American companies have a pretty dismal record when it comes to training and support; help your company be an exception.

Predeparture Training. Even the most careful selection and assessment process does not eliminate the candidate's need for some type of training prior to departure. The person needs an adequate orientation in the customs, mores, and attitudes of the host country.

Sending and maintaining expatriates overseas can cost organizations two to four times their home base salary. Several thousand dollars invested in predeparture training can save companies untold dollars in costly mistakes, yet only about one third of American companies provide this type of training.[11]

General Motors is an example of a company that provides excellent predeparture training. The GM program is for both employees and their spouses, and includes an explanation of all personnel policies, such as payroll, taxes, medical insurance, and relocation expenses. The whole family is then given language instruction (three to six weeks) and culture training (three days). If GM doesn't have in-house people who are knowledgeable about the particular country, it calls on American University in Washington, D.C., to provide instruction in cultural orientation and historical background.

It's important that the expatriate take this training seriously, and to a large extent that depends on your attitude. Convey the attitude that you want him to be an outstanding success in this assignment, and want to help in every way. And that means, give him time for the training. Don't pressure him to cut it short in the interest of "getting over there as fast as you can."

The training program might involve sophisticated methods such as intercultural experiential workshops, sensitivity training, or culture assimilators — but it doesn't have to. Experience has proved that the candidate will learn just as well by reading carefully prepared written materials that compare the United States and the target country in general terms — politics, economics, religion, and history — as well as specific aspects like food, relationships between males and females, and culturally appropriate gestures.

These written materials should also describe critical incidents differentiating U.S. and host-country customs. Here's an example: "When subordinates speak to their managers in the United States, they make short eye contact; in Korea, subordinates divert their gaze and make eye contact only when they are answering specific questions posed by their manager."[12] If you were sending someone to South Korea for two years to manage a new plant, information like this would certainly be helpful.

Send the Employee First. The usual practice among American companies is to send the whole family overseas together. But there's a better way: send the employee alone, a month ahead of the family. That way, she can have time to get settled in the job without the distractions of family worries. She can get acclimatized to the country in relative peace, and then will be in a much better position to help the family when they arrive.

Postarrival Training. Training needs to continue once expatriates and their families arrive overseas. Most companies continue the language training, but very few provide any additional cultural training after arrival. A big mistake! What better time to provide training than when culture shock sets in?

Mentors. A mentor, someone who knows the ropes, can be a lifesaver to employees and their families when they first arrive in the host country, and often thereafter. Sometimes expatriates find a person to take this role informally, but it's much more reliable when the company has a formal mentor system. The company links the newcomer with an old-timer, and the mentor knows that part of her job description is to help with the adjustment period.

Reentry Training. Every company needs to help its expatriates prepare for the readjustment. This can involve providing specially prepared written materials, counseling for the individual and family, or support groups of people going through similar readjustment. It's in the company's best interest to do this because it has a great effect on future recruitment of people. Unfortunately, reentry training is rare.

Who needs reentry training more, those returning from their first overseas transfer or those who have been overseas several times? The answer might surprise you. The more times the candidate comes back, the worse the reentry gets. Those who have been overseas more tend to do *more* discounting of the changes back home, and consequently don't take the time to discuss with family members how they all have changed.

MANAGERIAL SUCCESS POINTERS
Achieving Success in an International Environment

➤ Don't make the erroneous assumption that successful domestic performance will result automatically in successful overseas performance. Remember that success in an international assignment takes much more than merely technical competence.

➤ Use a combination of interviewing, psychological testing, and the assessment center to screen candidates for international assignments.

➤ Help facilitate the family's efforts to collect information about the assignment and the location. And spring for an expense-paid preview trip.

➤ Make certain that your organization provides a complete training program for expatriates: before, during, and after the time abroad. Don't overlook reentry training.

➤ Give individuals a month to adjust to the host country before their families arrive.

➤ Make sure individuals are clear about their major responsibilities and performance expectations.

➤ Make certain that your organization has a repatriation policy to look out for the interests of employees who are out of the country and ensure their position when they return.

EIGHT

Sharing the Gains of
the New Pay Strategies

The days of sitting down with your supervisor at the end of each year and finding out what salary increase will be added on to your base pay are coming to an end. The financial relationship between employees and the organization they work for is rapidly changing.

At the present time the base pay of many Americans stays pretty much the same from month to month. This typically continues until the next performance review, usually at the end of a year, when an increase is added. The monthly income then remains stable until the next annual review.

That kind of stable monthly income will not exist in the year 2000. By then, "up to as much as 40 percent or more of the average American's pay . . . will vary drastically from month to month." National surveys on current and future trends in pay practices across thousands of organizations are showing:[1]

• *Lower salary increases on base pay.* The trend is moving away from automatic salary increases based on cost of living adjustment or other automatic raises.

• *Less emphasis on paying the job; more emphasis on paying the person.* Most organizations base salaries on the type of job a person does. Job evaluation procedures often assign points to various jobs, based on the physical working conditions, the amount of responsibility and accountability the job requires, and perhaps the number of people supervised. Employees begin

161

to understand that the way to earn more money is to make the job sound more important than it is, take on more responsibility, or get promoted to a managerial position. This makes promotions too important, and puts too little emphasis on mastering the present job and too much on getting to the next pay level. In the future, more and more people will get paid based on the skills and knowledge they possess rather than the position they hold.

•   *More variable or dispersed compensation.* Organizations are moving toward pay-for-performance systems. They are carefully reviewing their performance appraisal system and their pay practices to make sure that a clear relationship exists between pay and performance over an agreed-upon period of time. The goal is to make compensation more variable between the better- and poorer-performing employees.

•   *More use of nontraditional pay practices.* The number of firms using such practices as gain sharing, department incentives, lump-sum bonuses or merit increases, pay for knowledge, and profit sharing will increase considerably.

There is some data to show that the companies that have been moving toward the nontraditional pay practices are becoming more successful than the more traditional organizations.[2] Jay Schuster and Patricia Zingheim in their recent book, *The New Pay,* predict that starting with the year 2000, organizations are going to experiment aggressively with pay strategies that reflect employee performance. Some of these changes will include:[3]

•   "Employees and organizations will become more closely allied and increasingly willing to help each succeed. The employee-organization partnership . . . will become a reality."
•   "Organizations will be taking a stronger role in helping employees acquire the skills needed for gainful employment. Training will be a universal organizational priority."
•   "Employees will develop the ability to perform a wider range

of needed skills in order to be of value to their organizations during times of change. Employees will become more flexible and more skilled."

- "Pay will be a positive force for organizational change and will facilitate making the time employees spend at work more challenging and interesting."
- "Although new [nontraditional] pay is not likely to be the only factor that will move us toward a more positive future, it is clearly the only way to make employee pay a constructive catalyst for this change."

Art's Story

Last month Art Berns had his fifth annual performance review since he started working for Computer Technologies Corporation (CTC), a national chain of computer stores. Art came to work for CTC immediately after graduating from college and is now a computer hardware sales associate in one of the largest CTC stores, with 150 employees.

Each year at this time, he meets with Cindy Peters, his department manager, to discuss his job performance over the last year, and finds out what his salary increase will be for the upcoming year. Last year he received a 6 percent increase, and most employees were expecting around the same this year. Art knows that to make more money he has to take on some supervisory responsibility. He is hoping to someday move into a department manager position and eventually to store manager — that's where the money is.

Next year, however, things are going to be different. Cindy spoke with Art about his performance over the last year and told him what his salary increase would be. But then she told him the news. Cindy explained to Art that CTC was changing pay strategies and that she would take some time and answer his questions now, but there would be a departmental meeting followed by individual meetings with each employee over the next few weeks. She gave him a sheet of paper outlining the five components of the new system.

Computer Technologies Corporation Pay Strategy

1. Base salaries will be kept small. They will represent approximately 60 percent of present salaries on most positions. In many cases this will be determined by a pay-for-knowledge system.

2. A second component of each employee's pay will be based on merit, reflecting the employee's performance over the appraisal period. This is a pay-for-performance program and will be in the form of a bonus, not part of the base salary.

3. The third component will be gain sharing, in which gains in departmental and store performance will be shared with employees. This will include a component for an individual's department and a component for the overall store performance.

4. There will be a profit-sharing component for overall corporate performance, in which a fraction of net profits will be shared with employees.

5. One-time, lump sum, short-term bonuses and recognition awards will be given for exceptional individual or team contributions.

The new pay strategy at CTC exemplifies a number of the strategies that organizations will be moving toward in the future. It is a complex system, because an individual's pay will be determined at three separate levels: that person's knowledge and performance, the department's performance, and the company's overall performance.

At first Art was overwhelmed. He asked Cindy quite a few questions about what these five components meant and how they would eventually affect his pay. Cindy took her time and answered all the questions. Art began to realize that he had the opportunity to make more money—and possibly a lot less!

In the new system, the employees are going to be sharing the risk of doing business along with CTC. Art is not much of a risk taker. The idea of perhaps making quite a bit less money for reasons that could be out of his control makes him nervous.

Strategies for Employees

Let's take a look at some ways that you — and Art — can achieve success in an environment with changing pay strategies.

Learn About Changing Practices

The first thing you need to do is educate yourself. Here is a brief guide to the new pay practices.

Pay the Person Rather Than the Job. More and more companies are moving away from annual percentage increases in base salaries. Some will grant increases only every two or three years. Other organizations will allow increases to base salary only on the basis of a pay-for-knowledge or pay-for-performance system.

- *Pay-for-knowledge, or skill-based pay.* You may eventually be paid by the knowledge and skills that you can demonstrate rather than the job you are doing on a particular day. This philosophy is often included as part of the team concept; an employee's salary is determined by the number of jobs she can do or the number of tasks she can perform for her team. If you are an engineer, you could be paid for learning customer service skills; if you are a human resource manager, you might get paid for learning accounting.

In this type of pay, your company offers you an incentive to develop skills that will give the organization a competitive advantage. You can increase your base pay by learning to perform a variety of jobs and making yourself more valuable to your team or organization.

General Foods and Federal Express provide two examples of the pay-for-knowledge or skills approach. A General Foods plant in Topeka, Kansas, starts all new employees at the same base pay and advances them a pay grade for each new job or skill they learn. Each new job is worth the same amount of additional pay, and employees can learn the jobs in any order they prefer.[4]

At Federal Express, all employees who have contact with customers must take job knowledge tests every six months. Those who do not pass the test are given extra training; they must pass the test before they can go back to their job.[5] The idea behind the testing is that employees are getting paid to possess the knowledge needed to provide the best possible customer service, and they are compensated for increased knowledge.

- *Pay for performance.* While pay for knowledge focuses on whether you can *do* a particular job, a pay-for-performance system focuses on *how well* you do it.

When asked, most executives and managers in an organization will say that they have a pay-for-performance system, when in reality they do not. When the increases are examined carefully, the high performers get only three-fourths of 1 percent more than the low performers. Most employees don't consider this a pay-for-performance system. Would you?

Art Berns was starting to realize how the various parts of the new CTC pay strategy were going to affect his job as a sales associate. He was beginning to like the idea of a pay-for-knowledge system. One of his concerns had always been that to make more money he needed to get promoted to a management position, but he didn't think he really *wanted* to be a manager. With the new pay strategy, Art could increase his base pay by learning the additional jobs of sales associate in computer software and purchasing associate.

This was a win-win strategy. It was good for Art, because he had a way to be rewarded without having to wait for a promotion. It was good for the company, because employees capable of doing several jobs could be used wherever they were most needed on any given day, making CTC more efficient and providing better customer service.

But while Art liked this new idea, he also knew that it represented only one component of his pay. The second part of the CTC pay strategy was what the company referred to as the merit component. It means Art is paid for performance. Art meets with his manager on an annual basis, reviews his previous performance, and then is given a bonus that reflects his accomplishments over the past year. This is a one-time bonus and does not become part of Art's base pay.

Paying for Group and Team Performance. Individual rewards are not the only component of the new pay strategies. More and more organizations are starting to reward at the group or team level. One common system is called gain sharing.

Gain-sharing plans are group-based incentive programs that share improvements in productivity, quality, sales, or cost savings in capital, material, labor or energy with the employees. Gain-sharing plans differ from company to company, but usually the cost savings are shared between the company and the team, department, or unit most closely associated with the savings. The formula or target that is used to calculate the incentive is determined beforehand.

There are two parts to the gain-sharing plan at CTC. Art can get a group bonus at the end of the year depending on how well the computer hardware department does. Also, all employees in the store can get an additional bonus if the store exceeds the prior year on several predetermined measures, including customer satisfaction and sales. Art is glad that this program is not the sole determinant of his pay increases. In some ways, his bonus is based on things that he can't control. He also worries that the high performers in the department would be making money for other employees who do not carry their weight. Nevertheless, as long as he is being rewarded for his individual performance as well, he finds the gain-sharing plan reasonable.

Paying for Organizational Performance. Another changing pay strategy among many organizations is to base part of an individual's pay on overall organizational performance. Two methods of accomplishing this are profit sharing and employee ownership.

• *Profit sharing.* When the organization is successful, it shares part of the profits with its employees. On the other hand, when the organization does not have a good year, there will be no money shared with the employees.

• *Employee ownership.* Many organizations are providing some form of stock options in order to create what one expert has called "a culture of ownership and caring." Programs vary widely in terms of how much stock is made available to the employees, but the idea is to "place some of the ownership of a company in the hands of employees."[6]

The final component of Art's pay was determined by the profits CTC earned nationwide. In a given year a percentage of CTC profits, if any, was shared with each employee. Art feels he has virtually no control over this part of his pay. And he's not sure about the bonuses for exceptional individual or team performance. He thinks they'll probably be relatively rare. But most important, after talking with Cindy, Art feels he has a pretty good understanding of the new CTC pay strategies.

You too must have an extremely thorough understanding of your organization's pay strategies. If you don't, your motivation will suffer. Seek out the specific information you need to make yourself comfortable. Do not be afraid to ask questions.

Learn About Your Company and Its Competitive Strategy

To learn more about your organization, make sure you read the most recent annual report, look carefully at the company's mission statement, and ask to see your departmental business plan and/or mission statement. Review your own job responsibilities and make sure you understand the link between your performance and departmental and organizational performance. Because your financial fortunes are going to be tied to your company's financial fortunes more and more, it is critical that you learn as much about your organization as possible.

> If the company is competitive — produces a quality product, satisfies its customers, keeps costs down, enters the right markets — then employees may reap significant personal financial rewards. In contrast, if the company makes mistakes — if it wastes money, if the product quality is poor — then not only will the company suffer financially, but the employees

will share in that suffering. While the average worker may not be involved in making high-level, company-wide decisions, he or she can have a significant impact through participation in decision making and problem solving at the work-group level. Work groups can address needed improvement in such areas as quality, customer service, and cost reduction.[7]

Focus on Your Own Job Performance

You may not have much control over your company's corporate profits, but you do have control over your daily work activities. Focus on your *own* performance; take pride in your work. Chances are, if you perform to the best of your ability it will not only have an impact on pay, but will also lead to the satisfaction that comes from a sense of accomplishment.

Plan Ahead for Uneven Pay

You are going to have to give a lot more attention to developing a personal financial plan. Because of the changing pay practices, you may literally have different paychecks from month to month. Therefore, you need to plan ahead, save money, and perhaps alter your life-style somewhat. Make sure you have money in the bank to cover your expenses in case a planned bonus does not come through.

In the past, Art always knew that whatever he was making in one particular year, he would make more the next year. This is no longer true. With the new pay strategy, he could make *less* next year than he is making this year. For the first time in his career, Art has begun taking financial planning seriously.

Ask for Periodic Performance Reviews

Because part of your pay will likely be tied to your individual performance, it is important that you know how you're doing. You want to make sure that there are no surprises at evaluation time, especially with a pay-for-performance system.

And don't make the mistake of relying on your *own* perceptions of how you are performing. Make sure you meet with your supervisor on a regular basis during the year, preferably every quarter, to review your performance. Ask for feedback. Make sure you ask for areas of needed improvement so you know which areas to concentrate on.

Take Advantage of the Opportunity to Learn New Skills

Many organizations offer employees the chance to grow and learn new skills through training and development opportunities. Take advantage of these opportunities, particularly with pay-for-knowledge systems; this may be the only way to increase your base salary.

One of the aspects that Art at first found scary, but later learned to appreciate, was the pay-for-knowledge system at CTC. Art liked the idea that the company was rewarding employees for learning. CTC called it vertical career growth — being able to make more money without having to be promoted to a management position. Art always felt he would like to broaden his knowledge of other computer-related products, so he began the training courses needed to be able to sell all the various computer software that CTC carried. He knew it would take a while to get the necessary skills and pass the job knowledge test, but Art was excited and his department manager was encouraging it. After all, the new skills were good for Art because it would increase his base pay, and good for CTC because it made the department more flexible.

Reach Out to Other Employees and Departments

Begin thinking about your job as if one of your responsibilities were to help co-workers in your own department do their jobs more effectively. Then look for ways to help other departments become more productive. Periodically meet with co-workers in your department or employees in other departments; ask if there are ways you could do your own job differently that would help them become more productive.

EMPLOYEE SUCCESS POINTERS
Achieving Success Amidst Changing Pay Strategies

➤ Make sure you understand your organization's pay strategy and how your individual performance affects your pay.

➤ Take advantage of opportunities to learn new skills.

➤ Learn about your company and its competitive strategy.

➤ Focus on your own performance and take pride in your work.

➤ Plan ahead for uneven pay.

➤ Ask for periodic performance reviews.

➤ Reach out and help other employees.

Remember: reaching out and helping other employees and other departments can in the long run help not only the organization but also yourself, when part of your pay is based on group or team performance.

Strategies for Managers

The changes in pay strategies taking place in many organizations are producing nervous employees. Your job as a manager is to take an active role in alleviating employees' concerns. Help them understand the system. Help them realize the advantages for themselves and the company.

Describe the Pay System Clearly. It is extremely important that you take the time to carefully explain the pay system to all of your employees. Even though there may have been direct communication from the human resource department, don't assume that employees have all the necessary information. Make sure that they understand how all levels of performance—their own, their work group's and the company's—affect their pay.

CTC held a communication meeting with large groups from the store; a written policy was handed out and explained to all employees. Soon after that, Cindy Peters, Art's boss, called a departmental meeting for her employees. She went over the new pay policy in detail and carefully answered all questions. She wanted to make sure that all the employees were clear on how the various components affected their pay. In particular, she wanted to stress the importance of working together as a team to increase departmental performance. She explained how departmental performance would affect the gain-sharing component.

Communicate Business Plans. It is important to get employees to focus on those aspects of their jobs that are critical to organizational success and, in turn, can lead to rewards for the employees themselves. As a first step, you must make sure that you clearly communicate business plans to your employees. Point out the corporate and departmental goals and objectives that the plan outlines.

Define Effective Performance. It is also critical that your employees understand how their individual efforts contribute to these business plans. Meet with each of your employees to discuss their major responsibilities, what constitutes effective performance within each of these major responsibilities, and how these tie in to the organizational and departmental business plans.

Cindy Peters met with each of her employees on an individual basis. When she met with Art, she discussed his major responsibilities and how they fit into the department's business plans. It was at this point that they discussed the pay-for-performance aspect of the pay strategy and Art's interest in learning the skills to become a sales associate in computer software. At that time he was only qualified for computer hardware sales. She wanted to make sure that Art had a realistic idea of what he had to accomplish and when he could expect a pay increase.

Relate Pay to Performance. Most people would agree that one of the purposes of a pay strategy is to motivate employees to perform better or learn new skills. If a pay change is to have an effect on motivation, your employees must see a connection between their pay and their performance. Be as open as you can in communicating how the system works. When employees do something particularly outstanding, the kind of performance that can lead to higher pay, let them know. In addition, if you believe it is important for employees to be willing to take risks, make sure that you are not always punishing failure. Reward "good failure" — the employee had the right idea or exhibited the right behaviors, but failed for reasons out of his control.

Encourage your employees to take on new skills. One of the more powerful aspects of a pay-for-knowledge system is that it allows you to reward employees for knowledge and skills that you believe are critical to your department and the organization.

Take Performance Management and Appraisal Seriously. As a manager, an important aspect of your job is to effectively manage and appraise the performance of your employees. You can't do that if you think of performance appraisal as a once-a-year chore that includes filling out a form, establishing a rating, and conducting a performance review. Rather, you should see it as a broad process of performance management, where you are continually giving employees performance feedback, letting them know what's expected of them, coaching and developing them, and clarifying how their performance ties into the various pay strategies. It's not a one-time event, but something you do on a continual basis.

Cindy Peters made a commitment to her employees that she had an open-door policy with regard to discussing their performance: they could come into her office any time they were concerned about some aspect of their performance or the CTC pay strategy in general. In addition, there would be checkpoint reviews with each of them on a quarterly basis, so they would have a clear idea of where they stood. She knew that several of her employees were working scared; she felt that the more feedback and coaching she could give them, the better off they would be.

Use Nonfinancial Rewards. One way to enhance motivation is to couple financial rewards with nonfinancial rewards.

Nonfinancial rewards can include informal recognition such as positive reinforcement, extra time off (permitting employees to come in late or leave early), favorable job assignments, or extra vacation days.

Involve Employees in Pay Strategies. When there is some flexibility in aspects of your pay system, ask for your employees' input. If your organization has a pay-for-performance system, get your employees involved in determining how their performance will be measured and linked to the pay system. Ask them what they think is the most effective way to evaluate their performance or to distribute merit bonuses in the work group. The more you can get employees involved in the system that measures their performance, the more motivated they will be to improve their performance.

MANAGERIAL SUCCESS POINTERS
Achieving Success Amidst Changing Pay Strategies

➤ Carefully explain pay system to all employees.

➤ Communicate departmental and organizational business plans.

➤ Define effective performance with each of your employees.

➤ Make sure your employees see the link between their performance and their pay.

➤ Take performance management and performance appraisal seriously.

➤ Make use of nonfinancial rewards to support the pay strategy.

➤ Involve employees in developing various aspects of the pay strategies.

Summary

The Six Keys for Success in Trying Times

We have written this book because we believe that there are definite actions that people can take to achieve success in today's trying times. As we look across the many solutions and strategies offered throughout the book, we find six common threads, six keys to success.

The Six Keys to Success

1. *Continual learning.* Obsolescence must become obsolete. Employees and managers alike must make a commitment to life-long learning—continually learning new skills, new knowledge and information, and new jobs.
2. *Empowerment.* Successful employees have the authority and responsibility to take action. They understand the degree and the scope of this power to act. They use it to help their internal and external customers, and they use it to solve problems and empower others.
3. *Role clarification.* The clearer the picture employees have of their role and the definition of success within that role, the more opportunities for success they have.
4. *Continuous improvement.* "Whatever you are doing today, you can do it a little better tomorrow." "If it ain't broke, you're not looking hard enough." "If it ain't broke, break it and make it better." All of these catchy statements mean one thing: employees can be more successful and they can make their organizations more successful if they continually,

patiently, and incrementally make changes to improve everything they do at work.

5. *Adaptability.* Some changes are good, some changes are bad, but one thing is for certain—change is a fact of life in today's organizations. Successful employees not only continually adapt to change, they champion changes.

6. *Self-understanding.* For employees to be successful in dealing with others, they need to understand themselves. Employees must understand their own attitudes and values because they influence how they perceive, think, and ultimately act.

Each of these six keys affects employee success in all eight areas that have employees working scared, but in different degrees. The table below shows which keys seem to have the greatest effect on success in the eight areas.

The Areas	*The Keys*					
	1	*2*	*3*	*4*	*5*	*6*
Less supervision		x	x			
Team culture	x	x		x	x	
Quality focus	x	x		x	x	
Downsizing	x		x			
Mergers and acquisitions		x			x	
Diversity in the work force					x	x
Internationalization					x	x
Innovative pay strategies	x		x		x	

We believe these six keys will continue to drive success for employees and managers alike to the year 2000 and the decade beyond. We hope the strategies offered in this book will serve to make you and your organization more successful.

Notes

Chapter One

1. J. S. McClenahen, "Managing More People in the 90's," *Industry Week*, 10 March 1989, 30–36.
2. Ibid.
3. Ibid.

Chapter Two

1. J. Schilder, "Work Teams Boost Productivity?" *Personnel Journal*, February 1992, 67–71.
2. J. Hoerr, M. A. Pollock, and D. E. Whiteside, "Management Discovers the Human Side of Automation," *Business Week*, 29 September 1986, 74, 76.
3. Ibid.
4. A. Bernstein, "GM May Be off the Hook," *Business Week*, 28 September 1987, 26–27.
5. B. Dumaine, "Who Needs a Boss?" *Fortune*, 7 May 1990, 54.
6. K. Murphy, "Venture Teams Help Companies Create New Products," *Personnel Journal*, March 1992, 60–67.
7. C. Larson, "Team Tactics Can Cut Product Development Costs," *The Journal of Business Strategy*, September/October 1988, 22–25.
8. A. Versteeg, "Self-Directed Work Teams Yield Long-Term Benefits," *The Journal of Business Strategy*, November/December 1990, 9–12.

9. J. D. Orsburn et al., *Self-Directed Work Teams: The New American Challenge* (Homewood, Ill.: Business One Irwin, 1990).

10. S. Buchholz, T. Roth, and K. Hess, *Creating the High-Performance Team* (New York: Wiley, 1987), 2.

11. G. M. Parker, *Team Players and Teamwork: The New Competitive Business Strategy* (San Francisco: Jossey-Bass, 1991).

12. B. W. Tuckman, "Developmental Sequence in Small Groups," *Psychological Bulletin, 63* (1965), 384–399.

13. Parker, *Team Players.*

14. I. L. Janis, *Groupthink* (Boston: Houghton-Mifflin, 1982); Parker, *Team Players.*

15. Parker, *Team Players.*

16. R. W. Wellins, W. C. Byham, and J. M. Wilson, *Empowered Teams* (San Francisco: Jossey-Bass, 1991), 22.

17. Michael Lovett, Piedmont Associated Industries, Greensboro, N.C., personal communication.

18. Orsburn et al., *Self-Directed Work Teams.*

19. Ibid.

20. Wellins, Byham, and Wilson, *Empowered Teams.*

21. "Teams Are Working Hard at Chrysler," *Production,* October 1991, 51–52.

22. B. Geber, "From Manager into Coaching," *Training,* February 1992, 25–31.

23. Orsburn et al., *Self-Directed Work Teams,* p. 40.

24. Ibid.

25. Schilder, "Work Teams."

26. Ibid., p. 30.

27. B. L. Davis et al., *Successful Managers' Handbook* (Minneapolis: Personnel Decisions, 1992), 70.

28. T. J. Peters and R. H. Waterman, Jr., *In Search of Excellence: Lessons from America's Best-Run Companies* (New York: HarperCollins, 1982).

Chapter Three

1. P. B. Crosby, *Let's Talk Quality: 96 Questions You Always Wanted to Ask Phil Crosby* (New York: McGraw-Hill, 1989), 181.

2. P. B. Crosby, *Quality Is Free: The Art of Making Quality Certain* (New York: McGraw-Hill, 1979).
3. J. A. Byrne, "High Priests and Hucksters: Do Quality Gurus Live Up to Their Name?" *Business Week*, 25 October 1991, 52–57.
4. P. B. Crosby, *Quality Without Tears* (New York: McGraw-Hill, 1984).
5. M. Walton, *Deming's Management at Work* (New York: Putnam's, 1990), 17–19.
6. A. V. Feigenbaum, *Total Quality Control* (New York: McGraw-Hill, 1961).
7. J. Bowles and J. Hammond, *Beyond Quality: How Fifty Winning Companies Use Continuous Improvement* (New York: Putnam's, 1991), 204–205.
8. J. M. Juran, *Quality Control Handbook* (New York: McGraw-Hill, 1951).
9. O. Port, "Questing for the Best," *Business Week*, Oct. 25, 1991, 15–16.
10. Bowles and Hammond, *Beyond Quality*, p. 33.
11. Port, "Questing for the Best," p. 10.
12. J. Carey, "The Prize and the Passion," *Business Week*, 25 October 1991, 59.
13. *Management Practices: U.S. Companies Improve Performance Through Quality Efforts* (Washington: General Accounting Office, May 1991).
14. Ibid.
15. Bowles and Hammond, *Beyond Quality*.
16. Ibid., pp. 26–27.
17. Ibid., p. 12.
18. D. Feuer and C. Lee, "The Kaizen Connection: How Companies Pick Tomorrow's Workers," *Training*, 25, (1988), 23.
19. *Management Practices*, p. 9.
20. Bowles and Hammond, *Beyond Quality*.
21. L. Dobyns and C. Crawford-Mason, *Quality or Else: The Revolution in World Business* (Boston: Houghton-Mifflin, 1991), 285.
22. Crosby, *Quality Without Tears*, p. 150.
23. Bowles and Hammond, *Beyond Quality*.
24. Ibid., pp. 133–134.

25. "Labor Letter," *Wall Street Journal*, 10 July 1990, 1; A. R. Kerr, "Executives Shift Blame for Declines in Quality, Poll Says," *Wall Street Journal*, 27 June 1990, 17.

Chapter Four

1. J. L. Mandel, "This Time, the Downturn Is Dressed in Pinstripes," *Business Week*, 20 October 1990, 130–131.
2. Ibid.
3. D. O. Heenan, "The Right Way to Downsize," *Journal of Business Strategy*, September/October 1991, 25–33.
4. J. Schwartz et al., "How Safe Is Your Job?" *Newsweek*, 5 November 1990, 44–47.
5. "RIF: An HR Challenge," *HR Update*, February 1991, 1.
6. D. Milbank, "Changes at Alcoa Point Up Challenges and Benefits of Decentralized Authority," *Wall Street Journal*, 7 November 1990, B1.
7. Ibid.
8. R. Henkoff, "Cost Cutting: How to Do It Right," *Fortune*, 9 April 1990, 40–46.
9. E. R. Greenberg, "Downsizing and Worler Assistance: Latest AMA Survey Results," *Personnel*, November 1988, 49–52.
10. S.W.J. Kozlowski et al., "Organizational Downsizing: Strategies, Interventions, and Research Implications," *International Review of Industrial/Organizational Psychology*, in press.
11. P. Ingrassia and J. B. White, "GM Plant to Close 21 More Factories, Cut 74,000 Jobs, Slash Capital Spending," *Wall Street Journal*, 19 December 1991, A3; J. S. Hirsch, "Many Bankers Lose Their Safe Havens," *Wall Street Journal*, 25 July 1991, B1.
12. J. Verity, "A Bold Move in Mainframes," *Business Week* 27 May 1989, 72–78.
13. Kozlowski, "Organizational Downsizing."
14. G. Salancik and J. Pfeffer, "A Social Information Processing Approach to Job Attitudes and Task Design," *Administrative Science Quarterly, 23*, (1978), 224–253.
15. D. O. Heenan, "The Downside of Downsizing," *Across the Board*, May 1990, 17–19.

16.   K. Cameron, "Downsizing Can Be Hazardous to Your Future," *HR Magazine,* July 1991, 85, 96.

Chapter Five

1.   P. H. Mirvis and M. L. Marks, *Managing the Merger: Making It Work* (Englewood Cliffs, N.J.: Prentice-Hall, 1992).
2.   C. A. Fink, "The Impact of Mergers on Employees, *Health Care Supervisor,* 7(1), (1988), 51–67.
3.   For more on the five stages, see D. Harshbarger, "Takeover: A Tale of Loss, Change, and Growth," *The Academy of Management Executives,* March 1987, 339–343; and Mirvis and Marks, *Managing the Merger.*
4.   Harshbarger, "Takeover," p. 341.
5.   J. A. Davy et al., "After the Merger: Dealing with People's Uncertainty," *Training and Development Journal,* November 1988, 56–61.
6.   H. Benson, *The Relaxation Response* (New York: Morrow, 1975).
7.   M. T. Matteson and J. M. Ivancevich, *Controlling Work Stress* (San Francisco: Jossey-Bass, 1987).
8.   M. T. Matteson and J. M. Ivancevich, "Merger and Acquisition Stress: Fear and Uncertainty at Mid-Career," *Prevention in Human Services,* 1990, 139–158.
9.   D. M. Schweiger, J. M. Ivancevich, and F. R. Power, "Executive Actions for Managing Human Resources Before and After Acquisitions," *The Academy of Management Executives,* May 1(2), (1987), 130.
10.   P. Pritchett, *The Employee's Survival Guide to Mergers and Acquisitions* (Dallas: Pritchett Publishing, 1987), 10.
11.   R. McGarvey, "Moving out and up," *USAir Magazine,* May 1992, 96.
12.   Schweiger, Ivancevich, and Power, "Executive Actions," p. 135.
13.   Mirvis and Marks, *Managing the Merger,* p. 328.

Chapter Six

1.   L. Copeland, "Learning to Manage a Multicultural Work Force," *Training,* May 1988, 48–56.

2. Ibid.
3. S. K. Kogod, *A Workshop for Managing Diversity in the Work-place* (San Diego: Pfeffer & Company, 1991).
4. Ibid.
5. M. James, *The Better Boss in Multicultural Organizations* (Walnut Creek, Calif.: Marshall Publishing, 1991).
6. L. Copeland, "Making the Most of Cultural Differences at the Workplace," *Personnel,* June 1988, 52–60.
7. Ibid., pp. 50–51.
8. R. R. Thomas, "From Affirmative Action to Affirming Diversity," *Harvard Business Review,* March-April 1990, 107–117.
9. K. N. Wexley and G. A. Yukl, *Organizational Behavior and Personnel Psychology* (Homewood, Ill.: Irwin, 1984).
10. Kogod, *Workshop for Managing Diversity.*
11. Copeland, "Learning to Manage a Multicultural Work Force," p. 51.
12. Ibid.
13. B. Jerich et al., "How to Manage a Diverse Workforce," *Training and Development Journal,* February 1989, 18.
14. C. M. Solomon, "The Corporate Response to Work Force Diversity," *Personnel,* August 1989, 43–53.
15. T. Cox, Jr., "The Multicultural Organization," *Academy of Management Executives,* May 1991, 34–37.
16. J. Smale, "CEO Column," *Meanbeams,* April 1988, 3.
17. Solomon, "The Corporate Response to Work Force Diversity."
18. Cox, "The Multicultural Organization."
19. Jerich et al., "How to Manage a Diverse Workforce"; M. Wiggins, *Workforce 2000: Sowing the Seeds of Change* (Chicago: Tenneco Corporation, 1992).
20. Jerich et al., "How to Manage a Diverse Workforce."
21. Jerich et al., "How to Manage a Diverse Workforce."
22. C. M. Solomon, "Work Force Diversity," *Personnel,* August 1989, 43–53.
23. Cox, "The Multicultural Organization."
24. Ibid.
25. Avoiding Rater Errors training, Human Resource Decisions, Inc., Akron Ohio.

Chapter Seven

1. P. R. Harris and R. T. Moran, *Managing Cultural Differences* (Houston: Gulf Publishing, 1991).
2. F. Elashmawi, "Multicultural Management: New Skills for Global Success," *Tokyo Business Today,* February 1991, 54–56.
3. Workshop conducted by D. D. Davis and B. M. Bass, "Adapting I/O Psychology to the 1990s: Meeting the Global Challenge." Society for Industrial and Organizational Psychology convention, Montreal, May 1992.
4. C. P. Early, "Intercultural Training for Managers: A Comparison of Documentary and Interpersonal Methods," *Academy of Management Journal,* 1982, *30,* 685–698.
5. J. S. Black, M. Mendenhall, and G. Oddus, "Toward a Comprehensive Model of International Adjustment: An Integration of Multiple Theoretical Perspectives," *Academy of Management Review,* 1991, *16,* 291–317.
6. L. Copeland and L. Griggs, *Going International* (New York: Random House, 1985).
7. Harris and Moran, *Managing Cultural Differences.*
8. R. L. Tung, "Expatriate Assignments: Enhancing Success and Minimizing Failure," *Academy of Management Executive,* 1987, *1*(2), 117–126.
9. Ibid.
10. R. L. Tung, "Selection and Training Procedures of U.S., European, and Japanese Multinationals," *California Management Review,* 1982, *26,* 57–71.
11. Copcland and Griggs, *Going International.*
12. Early, "Intercultural Training for Managers."

Chapter Eight

1. J. H. Boyett and H. P. Cohn, *Workplace 2000: The Revolution Reshaping American Business* (New York: Penguin Books, 1991), 117.
2. J. R. Schuster and P. K. Zingheim, *The New Pay: Linking Employee and Organizational Performance* (New York, Lexington Books, 1992).

3. Ibid., pp. 315–316.
4. R. B. Kanter, "The Changing Basis for Pay," *Society,* September-October 1989, 54–65.
5. D. Filipowski, "How Federal Express Makes Your Package Its Most Important," *Personnel Journal,* February 1992, 40–46.
6. E. Lawler, *Strategic Pay: Aligning Organizational Strategies and Pay Systems* (San Francisco: Jossey-Bass, 1990), 126.
7. Boyett and Cohn, *Workplace 2000,* p. 143.

Index

A

Acceptable quality level (AQL), 62
Acceptance, of mergers, 100–101
Accountability, for quality, 70
Acquisitions. *See* Mergers and acquisitions
Action plans, 19–20
Adaptability. *See* Flexibility
Affirmative action (AA), 112, 113
Ambiguity, 77, 79, 95, 96
American Management Association, 74
American Society of Quality Control, 58
Anger, 100
Annual report, 168
Anxiety, 1, 3, 6, 76, 107. *See also* Stress
Arthur Andersen, 130, 132
Assumptions, 115–117, 127
AT&T, 74
Attitude, 78–81, 98–99, 102, 103, 104, 106, 107–108
Autocratic leadership, 95–96
Avon, 124
Awareness training, and diversity, 126–127

B

Balance, in life, 97
Baldrige, M. C., 54
Bargaining, during mergers, 100

Barriers, and cultural diversity, 119–120
Base salaries, 161, 164, 165
Benchmarking, 62, 68–69
Benefits, 86, 130
Benson, H., 96
Beyond Quality, 49, 53, 58
Bitterness, 102
Blame, 104
Bonuses, 162, 164, 167
Bowles, J., 58
Business plans, 168, 172

C

Cable News Network (CNN), 150
Career uncertainty, 96
Catastrophizing, 98, 105
Cause and effect diagram, 62
Caution, and downsizing, 77
Celebration, 42, 70
Challengers, 25
Championing, of quality effort, 69–70
Change: demographic, 109–110, 112; involving employees in, 107; job, 102–103; organizational, 1–3, 92–94, 162–163; in pay practices, 161–163, 165–168; in thinking, 97–99; versus tradition, 140
Chevron, 101
Children, and overseas assignments, 137
Chin-Lor, D., 123
Chrysler Corporation, 22, 30

Citibank, 74
Coaching, 16–20
Coca-Cola, 132
Collaborators, 25
Commitment, 67–68
Commitment, to diversity, 123–124, 127
Communication: in diverse work force, 127–128; and downsizing, 84–85; and mergers and acquisitions, 105–106; of pay strategy, 171–172; and quality, 68, 71; and teamwork, 30–33, 68. *See also* Feedback
Communicators, 25
Compassion, 85–86
Competitiveness, 59, 168–169
Conflict, 95
Conformity, 125
Continuous improvement, 61, 175–176
Contributors, 25
Control, and culture, 140
Cooperation, 39
Cost of living adjustments, 161
Counseling, employee, 107
Co-workers, 30–34, 76, 77, 93–94, 170–171. *See also* Diversity, work-force; Employees
Crosby, P. B., 46, 47–48, 66
Cross training, 28
Cultural collision, 118
Culture: differences in, 112, 120–122, 139–141; organizational, 91–92, 93, 124–125; shock, 146–149, 159. *See also* Diversity, work-force; Overseas assignments
Customer-driven quality, 59–61, 65, 66, 70, 71
Cutbacks. *See* Downsizing

D

Decision making: style, 41; and work-force diversity, 115
Delegation, 14, 38
Deming, W. E., 48–49
Deming Prize, 54
Demotion, 79, 81
Denial, 100
Depression, 100
Deviation, quality, 64
Devil's advocate, 25
Differences, cultural, 112, 120–122, 139–141, 147

Digital Equipment Corporation, 123
Directiveness, and culture, 141
Disagreement, 42
Distance, between workers and executives, 8
Distrust, and downsizing, 77, 79
Diversity, work-force, 2, 109–110; and barriers to effectiveness, 119–120; case example, 110–111; commitment to, 123–124, 127; and communication, 127–128; and employees, 2, 111–120; and halo effect, 118–119; and managers, 2, 120–130; managing, 128–130; and motivation, 122–123; and performance standards, 114–115; and prejudices, 113–114, 115–117; and recognizing differences, 112, 120–122; and similarity, 117–118; and stereotypes, 115–117, 127; and training, 126–127, 130; valuing, 112–113, 123–124; and Working Scared Survey, 5
Downsizing, 2, 73–75; alternatives to, 86–88; and attitude, 78–81; case example, 75–76; and compassion, 85–86; and emotions, 76–77, 79–80, 85–86; and employees, 2, 73–74, 76–83; and information, 77, 84–85; and managers, 2, 73, 83–88; and productivity, 76, 79, 88; protecting oneself during, 82–83; reasons for, 74; and rumors, 76, 77–78, 83, 85; and Working Scared Survey, 5
DuPont, 74

E

Eastman Kodak, 7
Efficiency, increasing, 8
80/20 ratio, 64
Emotions, 76–77, 79–80, 85–86, 91, 100–101
Empathy, 33
Employees: assessment of, 71; and communication, 30–33, 68, 84–85, 105–106, 171–172; development of, 16–20; and diverse co-workers, 2, 111–120; diversity of, 2; and downsizing, 2, 73–74, 76–83; empowerment of, 28, 67–68; and feedback, 12–14, 15, 20, 68, 95, 169–170;

and mergers and acquisitions, 2, 92–105; and overseas assignments, 2, 134–151; ownership by, 168; and pay strategies, 2, 165–171; performance of, 11–12, 15, 70, 164, 166–167, 169, 172–173; and quality, 2, 57–66; and responsibilities, 10–11, 15, 29–30, 70, 79, 80, 93; and supervision, 1, 7–8, 9–14; and teams, 1–2, 24–35; training for, 28–29, 145–146, 157–159. *See also* Co-workers; Diversity, work-force
Empowered Teams, 28
Empowerment, 28, 67–68, 175
Equal employment opportunity (EEO), 112, 113
Equity, and culture, 140–141
Exaggeration, of negative events, 98, 105
Exercise, 97
Expatriates, 132
External customers, 60, 70

F

Fairness, sense of, 76
Family, and overseas assignments, 135, 136–137, 146, 147–148, 150, 154, 157, 159
Fear, 1, 3, 6, 76, 107. *See also* Stress
Federal Express, 22, 166
Feedback: and mergers and acquisitions, 95; and pay strategies, 169–170, 173; on performance, 12–13, 20, 95, 169–170, 173; and quality, 68, 71; and reduced supervision, 12–14, 15, 20; and teamwork, 68. *See also* Communication
Feelings, 76–77, 79–80, 85–86, 91, 100–101
Feigenbaum, A. V., 49
Financial planning, 169
Fishbone diagram, 62
Flexibility, 94, 104, 108, 135, 136, 148–149, 176
Flexible work environment, 129–130
Florida Power & Electric, 54
Flow charts, 62
Ford Motor Company, 126
Foreign assignments. *See* Overseas assignments
Formality, and culture, 141
Forming stage, of teams, 26–27

G

Gain sharing, 162, 164, 167
Gap analysis, 16–17
General Electric, 7, 22, 74
General Foods, 165
General Motors, 22, 74, 158
Goal orientation, 25
Goals, 101–102
Godfrey, A. B., 53
Groups. *See* Teams
Groupthink, 27, 115
Guilt, 101, 107
Gulf, 101

H

Halo effect, 118–119
Hammond, J., 58
Hand-off plan, 38
Herman Miller, 88
Hewlett-Packard, 126, 130
Honeywell, 23, 124

I

IBM, 74, 130
In Search of Excellence, 42
Incentives, pay, 162, 164, 165, 166–168, 172–173
Incremental improvement, 61
Individualism, 39, 125
Information: and downsizing, 77, 84–85; and mergers and acquisitions, 96, 104, 105–106; on overseas assignments, 155–157; on pay systems, 171–172; and rumors, 77, 85. *See also* Communication
Inner search, 135–136, 137–139
Insecurity, 79
Internal customers, 60, 70
Internationalization, 131–133
Interpersonal relations, 30–35, 37–38, 107–108, 118, 135, 136
Ishikawa, K., 49, 51–52

J

Japanese Union of Scientists and Engineers (JUSE), 54
Job: changes in, 93; compensation based on, 161–162, 165; enrichment,

28–29, 80; evaluation, 82–83; quitting the, 102–103; rotation, 29; security, 75, 76, 95
Johnsonville Food, 30
Juran, J. M., 52–53
Just-in-time (JIT) techniques, 53, 62

K

Kaizen commitment, 61
Kearns, D., 110
Kick-off question, 39–40
Knowledge, pay for, 162, 165–166, 170, 172–173
Kogod, S. K., 118

L

Lake Superior Paper Industries, 30
Language training, 128–129, 145–146, 147, 154
Layoffs, 73–74, 81, 86, 88. *See also* Downsizing
Leadership, 33, 95–96, 106–107
Levi Strauss, 130
Life-long learning, 175
Listening, 32, 34, 118
Logan Aluminum, 29

M

McDonald's, 124
Malcolm Baldrige National Quality Award, 54–55
Management: middle-level, reduction, 7, 8, 73; skills, 37–38; style, 24, 68; talents, 130
Managers: awareness training for, 37; and clarification of performance expectations, 11, 12, 15, 70, 172; and clarification of responsibilities, 10–11, 15, 70; coaching by, 16–20; and communication, 68, 84–85, 105–106, 127–128, 171–172; delegation by, 14, 38; and diverse coworkers, 2, 120–130; and downsizing, 2, 73, 83–88; and feedback, 12–14, 15, 20, 68, 173; and mergers and acquisitions, 2, 105–108; and overseas assignments, 2, 151–160; and pay strategies, 2, 171–174; and problem solving, 39–40; and quality, 2, 66–72; and supervision, 1, 7–8, 14–21; teams, 1–2, 35–44; training for, 37–38, 126–127, 130

Meditation, 96–97
Mentors, 127, 144, 147, 159
Mergers and acquisitions (M&A's), 2, 89–90; and attitude, 98–99, 102, 103, 104; case example, 90–92; and change, 92–94; and emotional stages, 100–101; and employees, 2, 92–105; and guilt, 101; and information, 105–106; and leadership, 95–96, 106–107; and managers, 2, 105–108; and motivation, 101–102; pitfalls in, 104–105; stages of, 91–92; and stress, 94–99; and Working Scared Survey, 5
Merit increases, 162, 164
Middle-level management, reduction of, 7, 8, 73. *See also* Managers
Minorities. *See* Diversity, work-force
Mission statement, 168
Motivation, 101–102, 122–123, 154, 172–173
Motorola, 64
Multinational corporations (MNCs), 131–133
Multiskilling, 28, 170
Mutual respect, 31

N

The New Pay, 162
Norming stage, of teams, 27
Norms, 34, 42–43, 124–125
Northern Telecom, 23, 39

O

Ohno, T., 53
Orientation, for minorities, 128
Outplacement assistance, 86
Overgeneralizing, 98
Overload, 79, 80, 94–95
Overseas assignments, 2, 131–133; case example, 133–134; company policies on, 144, 155–156; and cultural differences, 139–141, 147; and culture shock, 146–149, 159; deciding on, 134–139; and employees, 2, 134–151; failure in, 132–133, 153; and family, 135, 136–137, 146, 147–148, 150, 154, 157, 159; learning about country for, 141–143, 147, 157–158; learning about job for, 143–145; and managers, 2, 151–160; preview trip for, 143, 157; repatriation from, 144,

149–151, 156, 159; selection for, 152–155; training for, 145–146, 147, 157–159; and Working Scared Survey, 5
Ownership, employee, 168

P

Pareto, V., 64
Pareto charts, 64
Patagonia, 129–130
Pay strategies, 3, 161–163; case example, 163–164; communicating, 171–172; employee involvement in, 174; and employee ownership, 168; and employees, 2, 165–171; and financial planning, 169; and gain sharing, 162, 164, 167; and managers, 2, 171–174; and nonfinancial rewards, 173–174; and organization's competitive strategy, 168–169; and pay for knowledge, 162, 165–166, 172–173; and performance, 162, 166–168, 172–173; and profit sharing, 162, 164, 167; and promotions, 162, 166; skill-based, 162, 165–166, 170, 172–173; and Working Scared Survey, 5
Performance: appraisal, 130, 162; diagnosis, 17–19; and downsizing, 81–82, 83; expectations, 11–12, 15, 70, 172; and feedback, 12–13, 20, 95, 169–170, 173; and gap analysis, 16–17; overseas, versus domestic, 153; and pay systems, 162, 166–168, 172–173; reviews, 13, 169–170, 173; standards, 114–115
Performing stage, of teams, 27–28
Personal traits, 12, 13
Peters, T. J., 42
Philip Morris, 124
Politics, 95
Positive attitude, 78–81, 98–99, 102, 103, 104, 106
Positive consequences, 34–35
Power struggles, 95
Preferential treatment, of minorities, 114–115
Prejudices, 113–114, 115–117
Prioritizing, of responsibilities, 10
Problem solving, 39–40, 118, 127
Process orientation, 25
Procter & Gamble, 22, 124, 128, 132
Productivity: and downsizing, 76, 79, 88; and pay systems, 167,

170–171; and work-force diversity, 112–113, 115
Profit sharing, 162, 164, 167
Promotions, and pay, 162, 166
Putdowns, 31–32

Q

Quality, 2; accountability for, 70; benchmarking, 62, 68–69; case example, 56–57; championing, 69–70; and continuous improvement, 61; and customers, 59–61, 65, 66, 70, 71; development plan, 71–72; and employee assessment, 71; and employees, 2, 57–66; and empowerment, 67–68; and feedback, 68, 71; and managers, 2, 66–72; myths, 64–66; need for, 58–59; tools and techniques of, programs, 61–64, 65; Total Quality Management (TQM), 45–56; and Working Scared Survey, 5
Quality Control Handbook, 52
Quality Is Free, 47
Quality Without Tears, 47

R

Recognition, 42
The Relaxation Response, 96
Relocation, 79
Repatriation, 144, 149–151, 156, 159
Respect, 107, 127
Responsibilities: changing, 93; clarification of, 10–11, 15; delegating, 14, 38; and empowerment, 28, 67–68; and feedback, 12–13; and gap analysis, 16–17; increasing, 7–8, 79, 80, 93, 135; leadership, 33; managerial, 29–30; and overseas assignments, 135; quality, 70; and teams, 28–30
Retreats, 41
Retrenchment. *See* Downsizing
Rewards, 130, 173–174. *See also* Incentives, pay
Risk taking, 77, 86, 164
Role: ambiguity, 77, 79, 95; clarification, 175; modeling, 106
Rotation, job, 29
Rules, unwritten, 124–125
Rumors, 76, 77–78, 83, 85
Run charts, 64

S

Sadness, and downsizing, 77
Schott Transformers, 39
Schuster, J. R., 162
Selective perception, 98
Self-assessment, 71, 176
Self-Directed Work Teams, 36
Self-esteem, 79, 81
Self-talk, 98–99
Severance packages, 86
Shenandoah Life Insurance Company, 23
Shingo, S., 53
Singer Sewing Machine, 131
Six-sigma quality, 64
Skills: language, 128–129, 145–146, 147, 154; learning new, 28, 170, 175; management, 37–38; multiskilling, 28, 170; and organizational change, 162–163; pay based on, 162, 165–166, 170, 172–173 and teams, 28, 37–38; and workforce diversity, 126–127
Snapshot, of responsibilities, 10
Spouses, and overseas assignments, 136–137, 154
Standards, performance, 114–115
Star point system, 29
Statistical process control (SPC), 64
Status, and culture, 140–141
Steelcase, 88
Stereotypes, 115–117, 127
Stock options, 168
Storming stage, of teams, 27
Stress, 94–99, 147–148
Sullivan, K., 123
Supervision, reduced, 1, 7–8; case example, 8–9; and clarification of performance expectations, 11–12, 15, 70; and clarification of responsibilities, 10–11, 15, 70; and coaching, 16–20; and delegation, 14; and employees, 1, 7–8, 9–14; and feedback, 12–14, 15, 20; and managers, 1, 7–8, 14–21; and overseas assignments, 135; and Working Scared Survey, 5
Synergism, 23

T

Task orientation, 25
Team players, 25–26, 33–35

Teams, 1–2, 22–23; and benchmarking, 69; case example, 23–24; and communication, 30–33; 68; defined, 23; development of, 26–28; and employees, 1–2, 24–35; fear of, 36–38; feasibility of, 35–36; and gain sharing, 162, 164, 167; and ineffective team players, 33–35; integration, 103, 107; limitations of, 38–39; and managers, 1–2, 35–44; norms of, 34, 42–43; and problem solving, 39–40; and responsibilities, 28–30; and team-player style, 25–26; and teamwork, 41–44; and training, 28–30; and Working Scared Survey, 5
Teamwork, 41–44
Texas Instruments, 58
Thomas, R. R., Jr., 114–115
3M, 126
Total Quality Management (TQM): awards, 53–55; contributions to, movement, 47–53; premises of, 46–47; results, 55–56
Tradition, and culture, 140
Training: language, 128–129, 145–146, 147, 154; management skills, 37–38; and multiskilling, 28–29, 170; and organizational change, 162; for overseas assignments, 145–146, 157–159; and work-force diversity, 126–127, 130
Trust, 42, 77, 79

U

Uncertainty, 77, 79, 95, 96
United Airlines, 74
Universal Medical Supply, 132

V

Values, 113–114
Volvo, 30

W

Waterman, R. H., Jr., 42
Weyerhaeuser Company, 28, 132
Working Scared Survey, 3–6

X

Xerox Corporation, 7, 22, 69

Z

Zingheim, P. K., 162